Preparing for a Global Community:
Achieving an International Perspective in Higher Education

by Sarah M. Pickert

ASHE-ERIC Higher Education Report No. 2, 1992

Prepared by

Clearinghouse on Higher Education
The George Washington University

In cooperation with

Association for the Study
of Higher Education

Published by

School of Education and Human Development
The George Washington University

Jonathan D. Fife, Series Editor

Cite as
Pickert, Sarah M. 1992. *Preparing for a Global Community: Achieving an International Perspective in Higher Education.* ASHE-ERIC Higher Education Report No. 2. Washington, D.C.: The George Washington University, School of Education and Human Development.

Library of Congress Catalog Card Number 92-85442
ISSN 0884-0040
ISBN 1-878380-15-X

Managing Editor: Bryan Hollister
Manuscript Editor: Alexandra Rockey
Cover design by Michael David Brown, Rockville, Maryland

The ERIC Clearinghouse on Higher Education invites individuals to submit proposals for writing monographs for the *ASHE-ERIC Higher Education Report* series. Proposals must include:
1. A detailed manuscript proposal of not more than five pages.
2. A chapter-by-chapter outline.
3. A 75-word summary to be used by several review committees for the initial screening and rating of each proposal.
4. A vita and a writing sample.

ERIC Clearinghouse on Higher Education
School of Education and Human Development
The George Washington University
One Dupont Circle, Suite 630
Washington, DC 20036-1183

This publication was prepared partially with funding from the Office of Educational Research and Improvement, U.S. Department of Education, under contract no. ED RI-88-062014. The opinions expressed in this report do not necessarily reflect the positions or policies of OERI or the Department.

EXECUTIVE SUMMARY

With the world integrated by economics, communications, transportation, and politics, Americans increasingly see that they live and work in a global marketplace of goods, services, and ideas. Policy makers and the public want educational programs to reflect the international ties that bind people as they bind nations. Colleges and universities must produce graduates who know other cultural histories, languages, and institutions. American institutions must work harder to broaden understanding of world events by offering the perspectives of other cultures.

The challenge to educators is to deliver graduates who are competent not only to function professionally in an international environment, but who are equipped to make personal and public-policy decisions as citizens of an international society.

American higher education is meeting this challenge in many ways. Some institutions include their goals for international education in campuswide strategic plans. Others incorporate comparative and international assessments into individual disciplines. Core curricula are being altered to ensure that all students know more about the languages and cultures of other countries. Faculty-development opportunities are being created to help implement these changes. American students are being encouraged to study abroad, and foreign and American students with international experiences are being asked to bring their backgrounds to the fore.

Administrators are devising new structures for coordinating increased international activities. Many institutions are joining consortia to work on international projects with local, national, and international businesses and organizations; such programs increasingly are planned and assessed in a multinational, comparative context.

For consistent reference, the term "international higher education" represents international relations (study of relations among countries), area studies (study of particular regions of the world), foreign languages and cultures, comparative and international approaches to individual disciplines, and environmental, global, or peace studies, which examine issues affecting more than one nation. These education efforts can extend to every discipline and professional school, weaving together academic institutions, private nonprofit entities, businesses, local and national governments, and public and private international organizations.

In the 1990s, higher education has had to adjust to a more competitive world economy, increased access to and interest in the world at large, and globe-spanning electronic databases and computer networks. The decentralized nature of American higher education allows state and private institutions to make contact with educators abroad, bring curricula into consonance with job requirements, and devise ways to carry out the international aspects of institutional missions.

But other nations view international education differently. Shaped by geography and history, national concerns guide the responses of these countries to the content and form of international education. As colleges and universities worldwide expand joint educational endeavors, they influence one another's views of and participation in this field.

How Is International Education Included in Curricula?

Once focused on improving the international expertise of language majors and foreign-affairs experts, American colleges and universities now strive to teach all students about other countries and cultures. Language is not being ignored; standards for language proficiency are being tightened, and requirements for languages and study or work abroad are cropping up in professional programs (Lambert 1989). On the wider scale, institutions are revising general-education courses; for example, nonwestern countries get broader coverage in history and civilization courses. Depth and breadth of curricular applications vary, but this trend is evident among two-year, four-year, and graduate programs.

Throughout the curriculum, faculty are including material from other countries—books, films, videos, music, newspapers, even live satellite broadcasts. A few institutions make academic experience gained abroad part of the domestic curriculum by requiring enrollment in seminars, research work, or demonstrations of bilingual proficiency. Some offer certificates or joint degrees to students who complete a series of such courses.

It also is possible to have an international experience without leaving the classroom, thanks to advances in computer and satellite communication. American students now can interact directly with their counterparts throughout the world. Efforts to merge educational databases might improve access to research or curricular activities in other countries.

More faculty members are imbuing their teaching with an international perspective, but too few incentives are offered to encourage this approach. Faculty members who would like to see more international content in their work can use collections of course descriptions with international elements; these are published by single-discipline and professional organizations (Groennings and Wiley 1990).

Who Studies Abroad?

More students in higher education are studying outside their home countries. In European Community nations, student mobility is increasing; an ERASMUS project goal is to enable by 1992 at least 10 percent of EC students to acquire academic training in another member state. Educators and administrators at U.S. institutions want to match this goal, increasing the diversity of students who participate and the number of countries offered as choices (Burn and Smuckler 1990).

In a major U.S. government initiative, the National Security Education Act of 1991 tripled federal spending on undergraduate study abroad. The law provides more money for overseas graduate research and grants to support programs in international and area studies and foreign languages.

Analyzing study abroad from a cross-national perspective, institutions can compare the experiences of American students abroad with study-abroad programs sponsored by other countries (Burn, Cerych, and Smith 1990; Carlson 1990; Opper, Teichler, and Carlson 1990).

The United States draws more foreign exchange students than any country, but the numbers and destinations of foreign students are shifting (Chandler 1989). Asian students, who make up the majority of foreign students enrolled in U.S. institutions, are being wooed with some success by Australia, Japan, and other nations.

How Is International Education Administered?

Amid dramatic budget reductions, U.S. campuses are fielding demands for a curriculum more deeply infused with international and multicultural components, for greater access to study abroad, and for closer cooperation with multinational businesses. Institutions are deepening ties to institutions in other countries, coordinating programs through international-studies offices or campuswide committees, and cooperating with state and regional consortia (Anderson 1988).

At the international level, U.S. representatives are working with EC and United National Educational, Scientific, and Cultural Organization (UNESCO) authorities to standardize educational credential reporting, licensing, and certification. In a gesture likely to bring more students across more borders, these bodies are trying to ease student mobility across national educational systems and develop databases to facilitate exchange of needed information (European Center for Higher Education 1987). The EC leads efforts to create a comprehensive structure to administer international higher education (Luttikholt 1987). As higher education follows other industries into the global market, governments are looking with increased regulatory fervor upon joint educational business ventures (Chambers and Cummings 1990; Stein 1990).

How Can Faculty and Administrators Improve International Education?

The first step is to define the term. Clarify its meaning on your campus. Raise the concept on campus; see if "international education" as you understand it is backed by institutional policies toward international and foreign-language studies, foreign students, and faculty development.

Curriculum. Consider the extent to which your institution exposes students to other languages and cultures. Are international elements available even in professional schools? Do students acquire the foreign-language proficiency demanded in their chosen fields? Do all students get the chance to study abroad and to use that experience in later course work? Compare your institution's offering with those of colleges and universities in other countries.

Participants. Widen opportunities for international contact by reducing barriers to foreign study created by scheduling and academic requirements. Bring foreign students and teachers to the United States, and use international satellite and telecommunications in the classroom. Examine your own program in light of the efforts of other countries to send and receive students from abroad.

Administration. Evaluate structures that help or hinder international activities. Does a campuswide strategy exist to promote such efforts? Does a comprehensive document report these activities? Are measures of progress adequately communicated to the campus? Are course offerings, faculty hirings, and grant proposals coordinated with other institutions in your community, state, or region? Consider how other countries administer programs and how you might coordinate your efforts on an international scale.

ADVISORY BOARD

Alberto Cabrera
Arizona State University

Jay L. Chronister
University of Virginia

Carol Everly Floyd
Board of Regents of the Regency Universities System
State of Illinois

Elizabeth Hawthorne
University of Toledo

L. Jackson Newell
University of Utah

Barbara Taylor
Association of Governing Boards of Universities and Colleges

CONSULTING EDITORS

Philip Altbach
State University of New York–Buffalo

A. Nancy Avakian
Metropolitan State University

Paula Y. Bagasao
University of California System

David G. Brown
University of North Carolina–Asheville

Barbara B. Burn
University of Massachusetts–Amherst

Jay L. Chronister
University of Virginia

John W. Crewell
University of Nebraska–Lincoln

Clifton F. Conrad
University of Wisconsin–Madison

James Cooper
FIPSE College Teaching Project

Richard A. Couto
Tennessee State University

Donald F. Dansereau
Texas Christian University

Peter Frederick
Wabash College

Virginia N. Gordon
Ohio State University

Wesley R. Habley
American College Testing

Michael L. Hanes
West Chester University

John L. Howarth
Private Consultant

Joan Isenberg
George Mason University

Greg Johnson
Harvard College

REVIEW PANEL

Charles Adams
University of Massachusetts–Amherst

Louis Albert
American Association for Higher Education

Richard Alfred
University of Michigan

Philip G. Altbach
State University of New York–Buffalo

Marilyn J. Amey
University of Kansas

Louis C. Attinasi, Jr.
University of Houston

Robert J. Barak
Iowa State Board of Regents

Alan Bayer
Virginia Polytechnic Institute and State University

John P. Bean
Indiana University

Louis W. Bender
Florida State University

John M. Braxton
Syracuse University

Peter McE. Buchanan
Council for Advancement and
    Support of Education

John A. Centra
Syracuse University

Arthur W. Chickering
George Mason University

Shirley M. Clark
Oregon State System of Higher Education

Darrel A. Clowes
Virginia Polytechnic Institute and State University

John W. Creswell
University of Nebraska–Lincoln

Deborah DiCroce
Piedmont Virginia Community College

Richard Duran
University of California

Kenneth C. Green
University of Southern California

Edward R. Hines
Illinois State University

Marsha W. Krotseng
West Virginia State College and University Systems

George D. Kuh
Indiana University–Bloomington

Daniel T. Layzell
Arizona Legislature

Meredith Ludwig
American Association of State Colleges and Universities

Mantha V. Mehallis
Florida Atlantic University

Robert J. Menges
Northwestern University

Toby Milton
Essex Community College

James R. Mingle
State Higher Education Executive Officers

Gary Rhoades
University of Arizona

G. Jeremiah Ryan
Harford Community College

Daryl G. Smith
Claremont Graduate School

William Tierney
Pennsylvania State University

Susan Twombly
University of Kansas

Harold Wechsler
University of Rochester

Michael J. Worth
George Washington University

CONTENTS

FOREWORD

In the face of the breakup of the Soviet Union and China's preoccupation with internal affairs, the implicit demand on Americans to increase their international proficiency—thus strengthening our national security—has lessened. But with the decline of communism come other international changes, including the lowering of trade barriers, European economic unification, increased worldwide presence of the Pacific Rim countries, and a greater demand for free flow of people between countries, that might prove a far greater challenge to the welfare of the United States than any military threat yet experienced in this century.

It is important to realize that these changes are not separate entities; they interrelate in a system of dynamic dependencies that eventually reflect on every citizen in the United States. The impact of this interrelationship is not immediate, however; therefore, individuals are not keenly aware of the need to develop the sophisticated skills necessary to understand and cope with these changes.

In Peter M. Senge's recently published book, *The Fifth Discipline: The Art and Practice of the Learning Organization* (1990), he stresses the importance of seeing events in an interrelational or systems pattern:

> *Business and other human endeavors are also systems. They, too, are bound by invisible fabrics of interrelated actions, which often take years to fully play out their effects on each other. Since we are part of that lacework ourselves, it's doubly hard to see the whole pattern of change. Instead, we tend to focus on snapshots of isolated parts of the system, and wonder why our deepest problems never seem to be solved* (p. 7).

Because of the academic discipline and department control over higher education curriculum, colleges and universities are especially susceptible to this pattern of focusing on "snapshots of isolated parts of the system." Students predominately concerned with the short-term goal of graduation and beginning their first job fail to have as an element of their education strategy a vision of the factors that might influence their 40- or 50-year career. Consequently, the need to develop a greater international perspective—one that permeates the higher education curriculum—continually is underemphasized. Fortunately, many notable examples prevail in which higher education curriculum has integrated international education.

In this monograph, Sarah M. Pickert, associate professor of education at The Catholic University of America, first reviews many key curriculum reforms emphasizing international education. She then examines the dynamics and implications of the increase both in study-abroad programs and the number of foreign students studying at U.S. institutions. Last, Dr. Pickert focuses on the myriad administrative concerns of internationalizing an institution's curriculum.

We increasingly recognize the importance of international literacy or education in higher education; however, the value has yet to become integrated within the framework of the entire curriculum. It is the intent of the author to provide the background as well as specific examples that will help foster international proficiencies within every higher education institution—for every student.

Jonathan D. Fife
Series Editor, Professor, and
Director, ERIC Clearinghouse on Higher Education

ACKNOWLEDGMENTS

Barbara Turlington, Madeleine Green, Richard Lambert, and
Perry Pickert encouraged me to pursue a long-held interest
in international education and acted as mentors in this en-
deavor. The education faculty at The Catholic University of
America offered advice and support and gave me time to
think. Lisette Wright, Bharati Patel, and Christina Bolet spent
hours organizing and checking the bibliography. Marcia Annis,
Zita Kelly, and Dot Kane helped type, proofread, and print
the document. Norma McBurney made phone calls to track
down missing information. Students in an international and
multicultural education course commented on a first and
second draft. Anonymous reviewers offered helpful criticism.
Michael Dolan provided invaluable editing assistance. Finally,
the ASHE-ERIC office helped steer the document through
the publishing process and into its final form. Many thanks
to all of these people and to many others left unmentioned.

WHAT IS INTERNATIONAL HIGHER EDUCATION?

For colleges and universities in the United States and abroad, the concept of international higher education has evolved (and continues to do so), fueled by the interaction of individuals, institutions, nations, and international organizations. As referenced in this book, the phrase "international higher education" includes the study of relations among nations (international relations), particular regions of the world (area studies), foreign languages and cultures, comparative and international approaches to particular disciplines, and the examination of issues affecting more than one country (environmental, global, or peace studies).

These people embody the concept of international higher education in their capacity to function competently in an international environment.

* * *

The concept can take root in every discipline and professional school and is fostered when participants come from more than one country and when institutions have exchange programs, branch campuses, or other foreign affiliations—whether through academic programs or the increasingly dense web of transnational connections linking academic institutions, private nonprofit bodies, local and national governments, and public and private international organizations.

The goals of this field are different and change continuously as colleges and universities strive to improve students' knowledge of other cultures and their histories, languages, and institutions. One widely embraced goal is to produce graduates who not only are aware of the interconnections among regions of the world, but are willing to consider national perspectives other than their own. These people embody the concept of international higher education in their capacity to function competently in an international environment and in their ability to make personal and public policy decisions as responsible citizens of an international society (Hayden 1982; Klitgaard 1981).

Historical and Comparative Context

One definition of international education holds it to be "a variety of activities and programs designed to encourage the flow of ideas and people across cultural and geographic boundaries" (*Encyclopedia of Educational Research* 1982). Accepting this interpretation permits the roots of the concept to be traced back to the 336-323 B.C. reign of Alexander the Great, who established universities and libraries throughout his empire (Bozeman 1960), or to the reign of Emperor Asoka the Great of India (273-232 B.C.), who founded the University of Taxila (Brickman 1965).

Modern higher education began in the 13th century with the founding of universities at Bologna, Paris, Montpellier, and Oxford. In creating these institutions, their founders set the basic worldwide university model still extant, with modifications, today (Altbach 1991).

At the early universities, scholars sometimes segregated themselves by language and ethnic group, but the commonly held goal of advancing universal knowledge rendered their institutions international.

Since 1648, when the Treaties of Westphalia recognized the European State system of sovereign, independent, and equal states, international higher education has developed within national contexts. During the infancy of the American republic, their European forebears exerted a heavy influence on the new nation's colleges and universities. Students routinely traveled abroad to receive doctoral training, to learn medicine, and to acquire a taste for European culture (Veysey 1973).

But nationalism led some Americans to look askance at study abroad. Many civic leaders objected to the habit of sending young Americans off for a European education—a concern voiced by Thomas Jefferson in a letter to J.B. Bannister.

"An American, coming to Europe for education, loses in his knowledge, in his morals, in his health, and in his habits," Jefferson wrote (Brickman 1965, p. 29). But Jefferson was not concerned about adopting the European model in his own state; he sought French advice when planning the College of William and Mary and the University of Virginia.

The first colleges in the U.S. offered instruction in comparative languages and cultures, now considered a part of international studies. Initially founded to recruit and train men for the religious ministry, these institutions emphasized course work on the Middle East and languages of the Old and New testaments.

For example, shortly after its founding in 1636, Harvard College was offering classes in three nonwestern languages: Hebrew, Aramaic, and Syriac. Partly to stem the flow to Germany of Americans pursuing doctoral degrees, Yale University established doctoral programs in 1861 (McCaughey 1984).

International education has a far briefer history if considered as the role education plays in international relations. With the establishment of the League of Nations after World War I, politicians and academics hoped to develop a science of international relations that had a role for education (Scanlon 1960). In 1922, France and Belgium convinced other League members that education ought to be elevated from a domestic concern to a legitimate interest of international organizations, and the League created a Committee on Intellectual Cooperation (Kandel 1944; Scanlon 1960; Zimmern 1939).

The establishment of that panel helped international education expand to include such activities as improving the working conditions of intellectual workers in Central and Eastern Europe and supporting international exchange of teachers, artists, scientists, and authors. Other elements of this effort included international exchange of scientific publications, funding of research, and promotion of copyright agreements.

Eventually League funding proved insufficient, so the Committee came under French sponsorship. The body moved its headquarters to Paris and then to Geneva, reconstituting itself as the International Bureau of Education (IBE). It now is sponsored by the United Nations.

The U.S. government did not play a leading role in international educational exchange until after World War I. However, private American support for such activity dated to the turn of the century, when philanthropic foundations established by such industrialists as Andrew Carnegie, Daniel Guggenheim, John D. Rockefeller, and W.K. Kellogg endowed scholarships underwriting foreign study and international exchanges (Butts and Cremin 1953). Between 1920 and 1940, private funding continued to figure prominently, as foundations provided the seed money to create centers for the study of specific areas of the world, and international education became organized into area studies programs (McCaughey 1984).

Before World War II, a few foreign students attended American institutions. After World War II, however, students from other countries began coming in greater numbers and the National Association for Foreign Student Affairs was formed (Klinger 1965). It is known today as NAFSA: The Association of International Administrators.

With the signing of the treaties that ended World War II, sentiment again ran high in favor of finding an international solution to war. The founding of the United Nations and UNESCO brought hope that a world community would replace the nation-state system (Morgenthau 1967). UNESCO had as its goal the enhancement of international collaboration through education, science, and culture in order to "... further universal respect for justice, for the rule of law and for the human rights and fundamental freedoms which are affirmed for the peoples of the world ..." (Goodrich, Hambro, and Simons 1969, pp. 387-88).

Although it did not join UNESCO until 1957, the U.S. displayed a kindred spirit as it helped rebuild and develop European and Japanese educational systems that had been destroyed by World War II. International education became associated with government foreign-aid programs such as the Marshall Plan in Europe and the reform-oriented U.S. occupation of Japan.

Upon joining UNESCO, the U.S. spent nearly 30 years as a partner in that program's work to improve fundamental education, literacy, health, and agriculture around the world. American colleges and universities were enlisted to advise other nations on education systems, establish technical and agricultural schools in developing countries, and invest heavily in teacher training. International education became specifically associated with assisting developing countries (Laves and Thomson 1957).

The U.S. withdrew from UNESCO in 1984 over ideological differences, but individual Americans remained involved in UNESCO-affiliated educational efforts. Outside the United Nations framework, the U.S. supported educational programs and research by the Organization of American States (OAS) and the Paris-based Organisation for Economic Cooperation and Development (OECD).

World War II radically increased demand for international studies specialists, both in the short term for wartime service and in the long term for peacetime national security and reconstruction. In 1944, for example, the Rockefeller Foundation underwrote expansion by Stanford University and the University of California at Berkeley as well as the University of Washington of its Far East and Russian studies programs. Similar support came from the Ford Foundation and the Carnegie Endowment.

After hostilities ceased, private funding swelled in support of graduate and research programs. International education came to mean advanced training for specialists in fields vital to American security. With private funding on the rise and the Cold War heating up, international studies enterprise took off (McCaughey 1984).

Official programs began to proliferate within the U.S. government. Along with the State Department, the U.S. Agency for International Development (USAID), and the U.S. Information Agency, efforts to foster international higher education flowered at the Department of Education, the National Endowment for the Humanities, and the Peace Corps (Frankel 1965).

Congress stirred. The Fulbright Act of 1946, its purview widened by the Smith-Mundt Act of 1948, authorized federal exchange programs for American and foreign teachers and students. Not every such law arose wholly out of idealism. The Russians launched their Sputnik satellite in 1957; a year later, the National Defense Education Act was passed. Title VI of that act, which specifically supports language and area studies programs at American colleges and universities, remains an important source of funds.

As federal activities expanded, international education in America became synonymous with these U.S. government-supported activities. The government awarded technical-assistance contracts to universities for work in developing countries, funded the hiring of English teachers and agricultural experts, financed foreign-student scholarships, and established higher education programs for use by U.S. military and diplomatic personnel stationed abroad. The 1961 founding of the Peace Corps to send American volunteers to many parts of the world as teachers capped 20 years of increasing government support.

Expansion of American involvement in international higher education stopped with the war in Vietnam. As that conflict was souring the national outlook, Congress retracted from its formerly aggressive stance in creating new programs. The International Education Act of 1966 was passed but never funded. Federal involvement in international education began to decline (Coombs 1985).

Government's withdrawal was mirrored in the private sector, as the Ford Foundation rotated away from international programs to concentrate on domestic issues. American high schools, colleges, and universities reduced foreign-language requirements. Between 1967 and 1987, the ranks of language majors shrank by half.

The tumult that gripped the U.S. in the sixties and early seventies echoed around the world, as revolution and invasion cut off support for foreign-exchange students attending American schools. The U.S. academic agenda was racked by conflict over allocation of resources and access to higher education for minorities. International education eventually re-emerged, its focus expanded to include the issues of multicultural sensitivity, crosscultural understanding, and the environment, but much ground had been lost.

In 1979, President Jimmy Carter's Commission on Foreign Language and International Studies painted a bleak picture of American students' competency in languages other than English and their dim knowledge of world affairs (Pike, Barrows, Mahoney, and Jugeblut 1979). This report helped rekindle interest in international higher education, as did America's declining position in the world economy.

Current Issues in the U.S.

In the 1980s, a U.S. government eager to encourage private-sector involvement used Title VI to create a means of forming higher educational partnerships with the business community. Title VIB grants fund Centers for International Business Education and other higher education-business cooperative efforts.

U.S. universities often operate multiple programs in a single country. These activities can become disjointed because they are funded by different government agencies or by other sources. In 1990 USAID established the Center for University Cooperation in Development to foster relationships among American colleges and universities and those in developing nations, as well as to overcome fragmentation of effort.

The Center, which aims to broaden the areas in which U.S. higher education contributes to development, is studying the concept of creating a network linking institutions in developing countries to the U.S. Another project is the creation of enduring partnerships among USAID, American universities, and developing countries.

The end of the 1980s saw Congress resume its activist stance with regard to international education. Calling ignorance of world cultures and languages a threat to the nation's ability to lead the world, Congress passed the National Security Education Act of 1991, which increases the opportunities for American undergraduates to study abroad and increases support for training specialists in languages and area studies.

The law is timely: In 1991, fewer than 2 percent of American undergraduates studied abroad. The law also is a welcome source of funding; its $150 million trust generates enough

income to triple the number of scholarships for undergraduates to study overseas, to provide additional curriculum
grants to colleges and universities for international and area
studies and foreign languages, and to increase graduate fel-
lowship funding by 40 percent.

The American states also are taking action, prompted by
international economic competition. State governors endorse
international education as a way to bring more jobs and
income, by enabling workers to produce goods that are sal-
able on the world market. Governors want students to be lit-
erate, mathematically competent, fluent in a second language,
and knowledgeable about the cultures of America's trading
partners (National Governors Association 1989; Southern Governors Association 1986).

At the same time, states are strapped for funds, forcing colleges and universities to look to private enterprise as a bolster
for shrinking or vanishing government support. Their argu-
ment is that students who are better able to work in a multicultural and international environment constitute a sound
investment. And, as higher education follows other industries
into the global marketplace, the entire field is coming to be
seen as an international commodity offering the chance for
profits to countries and to individuals.

International Education and the Rest of the World
These changes are occurring around the world, altering institutional priorities in international work. Trends include diver-
sification of admission criteria, curricula, and types of degree
awarded (Cerych 1991). As higher education institutions
embrace the concepts of decentralized management, privat-
ization, institutional autonomy, and a tidal pull toward greater
access, all of these trends are influencing the national and
international relationships of institutions (Clark 1983).

For example, as different kinds of diplomas gain acceptance
as valid entry into colleges and universities, educators must
assess the impact of vertical articulation, in which more secondary students proceed to higher education. They also must
deal with horizontal articulation, or the shifting ties between
university and non-university sectors (Neave 1989).

Higher education institutions play a critical role in promoting internationalism, but that function is not prominent
in national goals set by most countries for their education systems (Eurich 1981).

Sweden is one of the few nations to have an official policy on international education. The Swedish Commission on Internationalization of Higher Education has as its goals awareness of global interdependence and importance of international understanding; building up of international solidarity expressed in the efforts and resources devoted to financial and other assistance to developing countries; and acceptance of the Western pluralistic value orientation (*International Encyclopedia of Education* 1985).

Since 1952, the Netherlands has made it a priority to address the urgent needs of developing countries, creating a special institution to educate foreigners. The Netherlands Universities Foundation for International Cooperation (NUFFIC) makes recommendations to Dutch organizations on international credential equivalencies, encourages academic mobility, and advises both Dutch nationals wishing to study abroad and foreign institutions seeking information about the Dutch system (Van Dijk 1985). Since 1970, NUFFIC has focused on a few developing countries (Enklaar 1985). Its NATURA network, based at Wageningen Agricultural University, provides a setting in which students from Third World nations can monitor development-related agriculture topics via satellite links and video (*IAU Bulletin* August 1990).

Although Canada ranks internationalism among its six priorities for higher education, the international responsibilities of Canadian universities are limited to supporting external aid programs. Nodding in the direction of internationalism in their higher education laws, France and Germany mainly reflect European Community policy encouraging cooperation; those two countries regard their "Europeanization" efforts to coordinate their higher education systems as a form of international education (Cerych 1991). In Japan, internationalization includes opening Japanese universities to foreign students and teachers and accommodating Japanese students who have studied abroad (Kitamura 1983; Mashiko 1989; Ebuchi 1989).

Although countries operate within national historical and political frameworks, each one encounters common international pressures: competition for the best students, calls for improvement in academic program quality, demands for high technology with which to conduct research and communicate, and the push for higher education institutions that can respond to international and global concerns.

American institutions face serious practical challenges in international education. The tasks involved include creating a curriculum capable of making all students more knowledgeable about the world; rewarding faculty who develop expertise in international issues; providing a high-quality education for foreign students that also enriches the campus at large; preparing Americans to learn and work in international and multicultural settings; and imposing coherence to disparate international activities.

CURRICULUM REFORM

Americans agree that students need to know more about other countries, but no consensus exists regarding the form such education should take at postsecondary institutions.

Institutions once concentrated on educating international specialists for particular professions (Newell 1987). Now Americans believe every discipline and career is affected by events around the world. This awareness has moved international topics from the academic ghettos of foreign language, area studies, and international relations into business, engineering, and many other fields.

However, despite a professed interest in other nations, American educational journals have been lax in addressing other countries' efforts in specific disciplines and in cross-disciplinary activities. These gaps are being filled: The *Chronicle of Higher Education* does a good job of covering general current events, and some institutions are subscribing to more foreign periodicals such as the *London Times Higher Education Supplement*, the *European Journal of Education*, and the UNESCO journal, *Higher Education in Europe*.

It is no easy task to change a curriculum at an American college or university to enhance its international aspects.

Curricular Change at American Institutions

It is no easy task to change a curriculum at an American college or university to enhance its international aspects. Besides the inevitable internecine wars among disciplines and a frequent lack of faculty with sufficient expertise on international topics, the administration often lacks the strength or will to guarantee the faculty a hiring, tenure, and promotion system that rewards work in international activities. Even so, many colleges and universities are developing exciting programs.

A useful frame described by Tonkin and Edwards (1981) reflects the administrative structure of most American higher education institutions. Existing structures often can be changed by increasing the number or types of required courses by requiring a foreign language, for example; by infusing international elements across all courses, such as by internationalizing reading lists; by altering extant majors, perhaps by introducing new courses or new emphases within a discipline; and by creating new majors, such as global, environmental, or peace studies, possibly reflecting an international perspective other than that which has prevailed.

In 1987, more than 75 percent of America's four-year institutions and almost half of its two-year institutions stated they are including some international component in their general education requirement (Anderson 1988). The most common elements are foreign-language requirements; courses with an international orientation; western history or civilization; world history, civilization, or comparative culture courses; and nonwestern history, civilization, or culture (Lambert 1989).

Course offerings vary greatly by type of institution. A taxonomy of 1972-84 undergraduate transcript data compiled by the U.S. Education Department shows sizable differences in the proportions of students enrolled in area studies, foreign language, and international relations courses by type of institution (Adelman 1990). Students took area studies, international relations, nonwestern government and politics, and foreign languages most frequently at doctoral and comprehensive universities; the exception was advanced Japanese, German, and classical Greek, which had substantial enrollments in liberal arts colleges.

Many possibilities for introducing an international perspective into the curriculum appear among the innovative approaches funded by the Education Department's Fund for the Improvement of Postsecondary Education (FIPSE), the Undergraduate International Studies and Foreign-Language Program (Title VI of the Higher Education Act, and Title VIB, Business and International Education Program), and the National Endowment for the Humanities. Many such projects and others are described in more detail elsewhere (Pickert and Turlington 1992).

Foreign-Language Requirements

During the seventies and early eighties, foreign-language proficiency among American college and university students dropped—the belated impact of an earlier movement among high schools and postsecondary institutions to reduce or eliminate the foreign-language requirement. Between 1967 and 1987, the number of language majors at American colleges and universities fell by nearly half (*Chronicle of Higher Education*, p. A55). A 1983 survey of entering freshmen reported that only 64.2 percent had studied at least two years of a foreign language before arriving at college (Astin et al. 1983). In the late 1980s, institutions revived the language requirement. By 1987, 73.4 percent of entering freshmen were reporting that they had enrolled in a foreign language during high school (Astin et al. 1987).

At the higher echelons of education, language studies have not proved as renascent. Today, only 7.8 percent of U.S. college students are enrolled in foreign-language classes. Lambert notes that colleges and universities have not responded to the often improved proficiency of entering students, continuing to offer most language courses at the elementary level. However, results of placement examinations administered to entering freshmen suggest that many students who studied foreign languages in high school still perform at beginner levels; of those who do enroll in postsecondary language courses, most do not continue beyond the beginner level. Even when they do continue, most do not become proficient language users. Most institutions do not offer enough instruction for students to work through the Foreign Service Institute's estimated hours of instruction needed to reach fluency (Lambert 1986). Many students who have become bilingual without formal instruction are not included in these studies.

With no comprehensive national plan for language studies, American instruction in this arena suffers from discontinuities among elementary, high school, and higher educational offerings (Lambert 1986). The Joint National Committee for Languages reports shifts in language entrance and exit requirements, increasing requirements for students wishing to become language teachers, language-teacher incentive programs, and support to institutions that assist local residents who speak several languages (Draper 1989).

Each state sets its own foreign-language requirements for public educational institutions; 17 have postsecondary foreign-language entrance requirements, and some now use as criteria not course work but proficiency. Some states, such as Colorado, require that applicants for foreign-language teaching positions pass oral proficiency exams.

Most institutions requiring a second language offer options. Students may exempt themselves from the requirement by doing well on the College Entrance Board's achievement or advanced placement language tests or by offering evidence of having attended a high school at which the language of instruction is not English. Other alternatives include study abroad, learning technical applications of a language, enrolling in linguistics courses on language learning, and mastering the ability to read a second language in a content area. When proficiency in a technical area is the goal, some institutions ready students for language examinations prepared in other countries. Students in Clemson University's Language and International Trade major prepare for certificates in business French issued by the Paris Chamber of Commerce and Industry and in commercial Spanish issued by the Madrid Chamber of Commerce and Industry (FIPSE 1986).

The Language Learning Course, a Boston University-designed cognitive approach, emphasizes second-language reading skills for learning-disabled students who have demonstrated through interviews and questionnaires that they would have difficulty completing a four-semester foreign-language requirement (Demuth and Smith 1987). The course goal is to help students develop an understanding of grammar, improve their ability to analyze language as an abstract system, and apply it to language learning situations.

As students study phonetics, morphology, and syntax, they are encouraged to consider applications to language learning. As a result of this experience, students report improved confidence in language learning situations and demonstrate increased language proficiency as measured by pre- and post-Modern Language Aptitude Test scores.

Some institutions do not consider foreign-language requirements the sole avenue to an international perspective. Rather than hire teachers for introductory language courses and insist on rudimentary language proficiency from all students, faculty at Lehigh University's College of Arts and Sciences recommended hiring more teachers in Chinese and Russian, adding upper-level offerings in other languages for students interested in advanced study, investing in a media resource center featuring satellite reception of foreign-language programming from around the world, and infusing international elements into courses throughout the university. A National Endowment for the Humanities grant helped Lehigh toward these goals (Pankenier 1990; National Endowment for the Humanities 1988).

Core Courses

Core courses are the heart of an institution's concept of what it means to be an educated person. Because these courses touch—or should touch—all students, changing their content or angle has the greatest possible impact of any curricular-reform initiative. After 20 years, many American postsecondary institutions are reintroducing core courses, including those with international content. Community colleges, criticized for provinciality of course offerings, are introducing international elements in their general-education requirements and coordinating foreign-language courses with four-year institutions so their graduates can continue their studies at a higher level (Greene 1985).

Using a "great books" or "great ideas" approach, history and literature courses can introduce international issues into the general-education core. The challenge to these courses has always been to treat key events in sufficient depth and context while offering a broad-enough perspective to widen a student's view of the world.

Rothney (1987) attempted this task through "Critical Issues of the 20th Century," a team-taught course that satisfies an Ohio State University history and society core requirement by following five themes: the world as an interdependent system (international); the heightened confrontation between "culturally conservative" and "change-oriented" societies (societal); the history of political institutions (political); the development of technology (economic); and the search for values for survival (cultural history). To adumbrate the traditional lecture format, professors developed laboratory assignments that included discussions of assigned fiction and films, interactive slide presentations, simulations, and debates.

Lewis and Clark College in Portland, Ore., links overseas study to a core curriculum. By participating in an "International Education/Core Linkage Project" incorporating several "inquiry courses" and by satisfying a writing requirement, undergraduates can satisfy core requirements while studying abroad (Burn 1991). This approach ties foreign-study experience more closely to the rest of the curriculum and encourages all faculty to consider the role of overseas study in a student's overall program.

Infusion Across the Disciplines
And New Degree Structures
Faculty can add an international element to traditional courses by adopting a foreign-language and culture component. When they are not language teachers themselves, some professors team-teach a course with a member of the foreign-language faculty or add non-English-language material to reading lists. Earlham College in Richmond, Va., has introduced foreign languages in several disciplines, including literature, philosophy, and history (Jurasek 1988). Four courses constituting

a Peace and Global Studies Series come from anthropology, political science, economics, and philosophy, and prepare students for study abroad by honing awareness of cultural perspectives, global dynamics, and the necessity for making responsible choices about issues facing the world community (Jurasek 1991). About 65 percent of Earlham students take at least one such course prior to departure for study abroad.

Brown University also integrates languages across its curriculum. French is taught in international relations; Spanish, in political science and Latin American Studies; Portuguese, in History and Afro-American Studies; and Russian, in Soviet Studies. Students concentrate on vocabulary and concepts specific to these fields. An alternative offered at Brown allows students enrolled in a French language course to learn discourse strategies useful in international relations and political science (FIPSE 1990).

Some two-year institutions introduce cultural concepts and technical vocabulary specific to their programs. Students at Joliet Junior College in Joliet, Ill., enrolled in courses related to the fashion industry learn differences in cultural attitudes toward fashion and color as well as specialized French, Spanish, and Italian vocabulary (Title VI 1989).

Other institutions create international education modules or units to be added to existing courses or taken separately by students from different majors and at several levels of language proficiency. The two-person language faculty at the College of St. Scholastica in Duluth, Minn., constructed a series of one-credit language and communication modules using French and Spanish in cultural settings. Units included interviewing native speakers, studying Hispanic films and songs, playing computer games in another language, and participating in language-immersion weekends (FIPSE 1989).

It also is possible to concentrate on one area of the world and treat it across disciplines. At the University of North Carolina at Charlotte, faculty from Engineering, Education, and Business Administration collaborated to revise their courses to focus on Japan. These efforts took place in conjunction with other institutional initiatives aimed at introducing Japanese into the University's foreign-language program and establishing agreements with a Japanese university (Title VI 1989).

Oregon State University is implementing one of the most ambitious programs—one that eventually will infuse each department with an international perspective by tying coursework to an international degree earned in conjunction with a traditional degree program. For example, a student earning a B.S. degree in forestry might elect to earn a B.A. degree in international studies in forestry. Encouraged by responses to a student survey, the university created an option for undergraduates in every field of study.

To obtain the international degree, participants must complete 32 quarter credit-hours beyond the required courses for the major, demonstrate foreign-language proficiency equivalent to that obtained at the fourth-year college level, spend at least one 10-week term in study, research, or work abroad, and complete an integrative senior project showing comprehension of global issues and the international dimensions of the student's major field of study.

The Oregon State program was successfully adopted in part because it does not infringe on the structure of the traditional degree. When faculty are not ready to endorse a complete infusion model, this approach might be an alternative. The students viewed the program as an enhancement of their credentials and future job prospects.

Disciplines

Another way to add international focus to the curriculum is through individual disciplines. This can be a beginning point for efforts to internationalize a campus: Before they can construct a program with an international perspective, faculty first must see how their own fields are influenced by international events and how researchers from other parts of the world view their disciplines.

In a National Council on Foreign Language and International Studies-sponsored project, Groennings and Wiley (1990) invited professional associations to solicit from scholars representing several disciplines articles on what undergraduate students in those fields should learn about the world. The resulting essays have been edited into a collection on international perspectives in geography, history, political science, sociology, psychology, philosophy, journalism, and mass communication. This publication constitutes a good overview of changes in these disciplines, and the following entries include some observations of those colleges.

Social sciences

Political scientists frequently provide an international perspective in courses comparing politics and relationships of various nations with other countries. However, Keohane (1990) suggests an inextricable link between international issues and domestic politics as well. He stresses the need for political science courses to be presented in a way that permits students to inquire about fundamental issues such as survival, war and peace, inequality, poverty, and power—all issues with significant implications for domestic and international politics. Only when students learn to resolve ethical issues such as defining the conditions legitimizing one nation's intervention into another's internal affairs can an international education be achieved.

Psychologists add cultural insight into explanations of individual and group behaviors by describing the impact of culture on cognition, perception, motivation, and interpersonal relations (Cole 1990). For psychologists interested in learning what is available, Torney-Purta (1990) compiled an annotated bibliography for materials to include in developmental and social psychology courses. Sociologists pay special heed to comparative applications of that discipline and concepts illustrating the interdependence of social systems (Tiryakian 1990; Wallerstein 1990). The American Sociological Association published a collection of sociology course syllabi with an international component (Goodman, Armer, and Carlson 1991).

Foreign languages

Language departments now integrate culture into their instruction (Crawford-Lange and Lange 1984), incorporating discussion of relevant topics such as geography and political and legal systems (Leaver and Stryker 1989). These departments have increased their emphasis on oral and written proficiency (Freed 1989) and redesigned the curriculum for foreign-language teachers (Moeller 1989).

The cultural content of language courses typically appears as notes, pictures and illustrations, literature (including prose, poetry, and proverbs), games, songs, films, and role-playing exercises. Crawford-Lange and Lange (1984) argue that in most language classrooms, the differences in cultural attitudes and conventions remain a peripheral goal. They urge that language be taught in the context of a cultural issue familiar to students.

For example, by exploring the themes of assessing chances for employment or attending school in another culture, students can deal with statistics on minimum wages, rules about school discipline, and attendance codes. After discussing their initial perceptions of these themes, students can consider what they need in terms of language function, structure, syntax, registers, and vocabulary to continue discussing the subject. In this way, the theoretical meets the practical. For example, as one who is looking for work in France, how do you address a potential employer? Next, students examine the cultural differences they have uncovered and discuss the reasons why those differences exist. With this approach, instructors evaluate students on proficiency in both language and cultural understanding by requiring conversations and written material in the target language.

Some institutions use computers, videodiscs, and satellite technology to enhance language learning. "In the French Body," a course created with a computer program and a videodisc, helps students concentrate on nonverbal aspects of communication such as facial expression and gesture as well as grammar and vocabulary. Students enrolled in "Body" watch tapes of 60-second unscripted conversations between native French speakers, and then act out these conversations (FIPSE 1990).

Many institutions would like to use direct satellite broadcasts in language instruction, but often these require supplemental material that is difficult or costly to obtain. "France-TV," a monthly language and culture video magazine compiled at the University of Maryland's Baltimore County campus, covers cultural, political, and current events using excerpts from French broadcasts. Complete transcription and teaching materials on ways to use the broadcasts supplement the videos (FIPSE 1990).

Physical and natural sciences
Science and mathematics pose the greatest challenge to advocates of the international perspective in higher education. Some institutions incorporate language into science courses, encouraging study abroad and offering certificates for enrolling in a sequence of designated courses oriented to international topics. At St. Olaf College in Northfield, Minn., mathematics and natural and behavioral science majors earn an Applied Foreign Language Component certificate by completing an advanced foreign series. Certificates are granted to students completing two of the following: a regular course

in which approximately half the readings and other assignments are in a foreign language; a disciplinary guided reading course in a foreign language; an internship abroad that requires a second language; or a science course taught in a foreign language on campus or as part of a foreign-study program. Math and science majors also can opt for an English-only or a foreign-language track. On the language route, half the text material is in French, Spanish, or German, with a quarter of class sessions conducted by a language teacher in the foreign tongue (FIPSE 1989).

Interdisciplinary Approaches

Area studies
An international perspective can evolve by focusing on a single geographical region with a distinct culture. Reports on teaching about particular countries, such as a German Marshall Fund study of contemporary Germany in the U.S., or a study of the teaching of Japanese in the U.S., help reveal the status of teaching and research of a particular region or country. These reports describe the state of course offerings about that nation in language, history, social sciences, and professional schools (Janes and Scher 1987; Japan Foundation 1989).

Sometimes an interest in area studies emerges at an institution because of location or students' cultural backgrounds. *Cultura e Commercio,* a program in language, liberal arts, and commerce developed at State University of New York Staten Island, focuses on Italy—an inherently appealing subject in light of the ancestry of many students at this institution. Students gain fluency in Italian, then declare an Arts and Science major in art, economics, English, history, international studies, or political science—subsequently enrolling in a sequence of international-business courses and spending part of the junior year in Florence. Seniors participate in program-arranged internships with Italian or Italian-American firms (FIPSE 1987).

International relations
Some in this field claim American social science conceptual frameworks dominate the discipline, but others deny a skew toward the U.S. or any other country. A Ford Foundation report covering studies in Britain, France, Germany, Netherlands, Sweden, and Italy illustrates the extent to which inter-

pretations vary on the scope of the subject and its methodology (Ford Foundation 1976). Researchers agree that interstate relations now are only one of many systems of international relations being studied (Palmer 1980). However, it is difficult to summarize trends in this arena, since faculty in many countries have individual research agendas, frustrating analysts.

Global education

A grass-roots movement dating to the late 1970s, global education has become a catchphrase often used synonymously with international relations, area studies, and peace and world order studies, or with single issues such as world hunger and global warming (Vocke 1988).

Most global educators say the growth of international economic and political systems, demographic shifts, and a declining American hegemony have accelerated global interdependence. They urge academicians, politicians, business people, and citizens to see past national borders and prepare to deal in world terms (Anderson 1991).

Peace studies

In 1984, the U.S. moved to expand knowledge about the nature of war and peace by establishing the United States Institute of Peace (Lewis 1989). In 1989, the American Academy of Political and Social Science dedicated a special issue to the 40th anniversary of peace studies in the U.S. (Lopez 1989). This field continues to focus on causes and consequences of violent conflict; ways to manage, reduce, or resolve violent conflict; and values, norms, and institutions for building peace. Collections of curricular guides on courses covering peace and world order show how faculty address these issues in individual courses (Wien 1981).

Comparatively speaking, peace education is central to the Finnish concept of internationalism. There, peace studies as a topic is blended into courses on political science, sociology, social psychology, communications sciences, history, and teacher training (Kyllonen 1984).

Ethnic/multicultural studies

International and multicultural educators share an interest in educating students about cultures of the world and in cross-cultural understanding. Current publications encourage faculty

International and multicultural educators share an interest in educating students about cultures of the world and in cross-cultural understanding.

to broaden the scope of course material in this direction. The tendency of Black Studies courses to focus on the Pan-African world, for example, means that the wider Third World, which also has cultural ties to African Americans, sometimes is overlooked (Edmondson 1984). Georgia Southern University is strengthening its African and African-American Studies program beyond a traditional focus on sub-Saharan Africa to offer Caribbean and African Literature in French (1991).

Institutions desiring to incorporate the multilingual and multicultural expertise of students into international educational efforts sometimes turn to local refugee and immigrant communities. California State University at Stanislaus engages university students from anthropology, education, nursing, and social work in a set of field-work experiences with Cambodian refugees. A language and cultural immersion course is taught at the field site, using native speakers as tutors. Students also may enroll in a course on intercultural communication (FIPSE 1990).

Professional Schools
Business
Urged on by professional accrediting organizations and encouraged by new federal funding, business schools are increasing their international curriculum by revising courses, establishing new majors, and creating centers for international business education. Accounting courses now include instruction on analyzing foreign financial statements and calculating foreign currency conversions (Laribee 1988; Ramaglia 1988). Finance courses offer practice in analyzing international financial markets (Garg 1987).

In 1989, the U.S. Education Department began Title VIB programs to encourage cooperation among business schools, other university segments, and the business community through Centers for International Business Education (CIBE). The University of Michigan School of Business Administration established one of 16 such centers. Acting as a regional and national resource for the academic, business, and professional communities, it sponsors faculty seminars that bring together business and nonbusiness faculty, also providing outreach programs to the community and collaborating on projects with community colleges (Title VIB 1990).

Education and social work

Education majors are among the least likely of students to enroll in courses with an international emphasis (Lambert 1989). Like other professional schools, some education programs encourage students to engage in practical internship experiences in other countries. Some programs permit students to complete their student teaching in English-speaking schools located abroad (West 1985). Case studies of teacher-education programs that are especially active in global activities describe numerous approaches to making the discipline more international (Florida International University: Lafayette 1985; Indiana University: Ochoa 1986; Northern Illinois University: Gueulette 1987).

However, in a 1990 survey of schools of education that prepare high school social-studies teachers to teach with a global perspective, many programs were found not to emphasize a historical approach to international topics. They also omitted discussions of worldwide environmental issues (Merryfield 1991).

The internationalization of social-work practice requires that social workers be familiar with other countries' political, legal, and social-welfare systems, as well as U.S. policies on such topics as international adoption and settlement of refugee minors. In response, social-work professional groups produced a manual to help faculty incorporate international content into their courses (Healy, n.d.). Curriculum modules introduce students to global aspects of poverty and hunger, children's rights, and intercountry adoption.

Mining and engineering

Aware that 70 percent of engineering services provided in the U.S. encounter international competition, the Colorado School of Mines moved to prepare its students for the real work by creating a department of global systems and cultures and a minor in international political economy within its engineering school. Students enroll in social-science courses that focus on Latin America or Asia, studying the language of the country in which they will complete a field practicum as practicing engineers. While travel costs restrict student participation in foreign internships, the school has identified private and state-owned enterprises to underwrite the cost of room and board and to provide a small stipend (FIPSE 1989; Goodwin and Nacht 1991).

The University of Rhode Island adds an international approach to engineering by encouraging students to complete two degrees: the first a B.S. in any of the traditional engineering areas, the second a B.A. in German that requires intensive German language courses and an advanced engineering course taught in German by engineering faculty. An international engineering internship program enrolls participants in intensive German language courses for engineers prior to work with a German engineering firm (FIPSE 1990).

Simulations

For many years colleges and universities have used simulations, role-playing activities, debates, and similar means to encourage student involvement in many disciplines. Telecommunications advances now make it possible for simulations to cross national boundaries, making their membership as well as their content international. These encounters partially make up for gaps in the experience of students who do not go abroad and who lack substantial academic contact with people from other countries.

In simulations, high school and postsecondary students communicate electronically with partners in other countries through such exercises as a month-long program coordinated by the University of Maryland. Called ICONS, this project links teams of students from many U.S. institutions with each other and with students in Argentina, Germany, and Japan. Using simulation software, students use personal computers and modems to gain access to communications networks such as Telenet and NSFNET, then debate international issues such as arms control, European economic unification, the Middle East, human rights, Third World economic development, and the global environment (Wilkenfeld 1983).

International Baccalaureate

Few educators advocate a curriculum that could be acceptable worldwide. One exception is the International Baccalaureate, used in high schools around the world and accepted as equivalent to one year of postsecondary education in many countries (Freeman 1987; Peterson 1972; Fox 1985). Established in 1960 to meet the needs of expatriate students who attended secondary school in one country and higher education in another, the curriculum is divided into languages, the study of man, experimental sciences, mathematics, and the arts.

Graduates must pass a comprehensive examination. The International Baccalaureate Organization (IBO) responded to criticism that the curriculum was too heavily western by allowing institutions greater flexibility in the courses they offer.

Curricula for Foreign Students

Discussions of international-studies curricula rarely address the appropriate form and content of a curriculum for foreign students in U.S. institutions. American colleges and universities want to broaden the intellectual horizons of all students, but many believe that of itself an American education is sufficiently international for foreign students. Classes offered specifically for foreign students generally introduce these students to the American political and education system and instruct them in English as a second language (Will 1980). Through a USIA-funded program, NAFSA encourages institutions to provide ways for foreign students to participate in community activities and many other projects to learn more about the U.S. and teach Americans about their native lands.

Important questions remain about the curriculum for foreign students. Many have come to the U.S. seeking specific technical and professional knowledge. Should foreign students be required to learn about countries other than the U.S.? Must they be encouraged to enroll in study-abroad programs? Do they need to be integrated into advanced language courses or offered special classes for themselves?

Academic Achievement and Curriculum Evaluation

Interest in assessing college students' knowledge of and attitudes about people in other countries began in the 1980s, when the Educational Testing Service and the Council on Learning constructed the college-level Survey of Global Awareness (Black and Bonham 1981a). Scholars from the disciplines of world history, sociology, international economics, and international relations composed questions on historical periods and geographical areas. The instrument was not fully implemented, but the pilot data from 3,000 American freshmen and seniors was disappointing. Subjects typically answered correctly on only half of the 101 test items.

To gauge knowledge of language and international affairs gained in high school language and history courses, ETS turned to its advanced placement exam format. The firm also is developing test items for a political science examination

(FIPSE 1989). As advanced placement tests are more widely recognized as measuring mastery of college-level material, they become the measure of what Americans believe college students should know about these subjects.

Save for its informal demonstration of American student ignorance on international issues, the original ETS Survey of Global Awareness has not been used widely, but Japanese researchers expressed an interest in a comparative study using this test. In the 1980s the instrument was modified, translated into Japanese, and back-translated to assure accuracy. After requesting background information on respondents—such as foreign-language proficiency—the test asked students to agree or disagree with statements about human rights, world government, cooperation, and war, and then posed questions to measure participants' interest in other parts of the world. Finally, participants were tested through multiple-choice questions on their knowledge of the world. Cogan, Torney-Purta, and Anderson (1988) administered the test to some 1,300 Japanese public university freshmen and senior education majors.

Japanese students enter the university relatively more knowledgeable about the world than American freshmen, but their knowledge increases only slightly over four years. Japanese freshmen had higher test scores than their American counterparts, but by senior year these differences had disappeared. American seniors knew as much as Japanese seniors, whose scores were only slightly above their freshman sample.

On attitude items, Americans were far more likely to agree with the statement, "Studying a foreign language can be important for me because other people will respect me more if I have knowledge of a foreign language." Concerning war and human rights, about half the American students agreed that "under some conditions war is necessary to maintain justice," compared with less than eight percent of the Japanese. Only 13 percent of American students agreed that "People should refuse to engage in any war, no matter how serious the consequences to their country," while 78 percent of Japanese students agreed.

At the national level, more interest abounds in collecting educational achievement measures through international organizations and joint national projects (Torney-Purta 1990; Walberg 1990). To publicize expectations of other countries about what their students should know about world history and geography, the National Endowment for the Humanities published examples of questions taken from national tests for the French baccalaureate, the General Certificate of Secondary Education for England and Wales, the German Abitur, and the European baccalauréat examination for European Community schools in Brussels.

European students seem to be required to know much more about world history than students in the U.S. The National Endowment questioned whether American students could pass the French test on U.S foreign policy or a British test requiring a detailed understanding of American progressivism. Similarly, the Endowment wondered whether American teachers require their students to know the history of other countries in the same detail that other countries do (National Endowment for the Humanities 1991).

The evaluation of individual courses for their international content depends on the objectives for each course. To assist teachers who use common frameworks, Torney-Purta (1989) created a format for evaluating five approaches to world studies: world history, western civilization, historical cultures, world geography, and international relations. She suggests that evaluators decide if a curriculum actually has been implemented, then assess knowledge and skill acquisition specific to the approach used (criterion-referenced, multiple-choice, and open-ended tests). Torney-Purta discusses secondary-school curricula, but the evaluation strategies have general application.

Summary and Research Needed on International Curricula
American strengths
Curricula in American higher education institutions carry a high value worldwide, evidenced by the number of foreign students who come to the U.S. to study. Paradoxically, when asked to define an international education curriculum, many institutions voice doubt about the adequacy of today's offerings. As a result, colleges and universities are introducing information about other countries into individual courses and infusing international components across the curriculum in every major and at every level. A lack of consensus on how to proceed permits institutions to match curricular changes with students' perceived needs, such as increasing demand for spoken proficiency in two languages and knowledge about

parts of the world as they relate to future careers.

Advances in telecommunications and computers permit creation of courses in which students in the U.S. communicate directly with people elsewhere without traveling any farther than a telephone, computer terminal, or television.

American weaknesses

Because no unified approach to curricular change exists in American higher education, many gaps remain in course and program content and quality. Relatively little information on how other countries approach the topic or even on the curriculum for foreign students in American institutions is applied practically. This difficulty stems partly from American educators' lack of proficiency in languages other than English.

Research needed

At the local level, how does curricular change affect the average college or university student? What have foreign students learned in the U.S.? What is the impact at the national level of curriculum improvement projects on career choices, faculty research, or program offerings? What knowledge about the world do American students lack that college and university students in other countries possess? Are there ways the federal government could help American institutions use technology to improve interaction with institutions and data banks in other countries?

At the international level, what curricular activities do international organizations promote and how can American institutions use them successfully?

EDUCATIONAL MOBILITY: Study-Abroad and Foreign Students

Study Abroad

After language instruction, study abroad is the most common feature of international-studies programs on American campuses (Lambert 1989). Many governments view study-abroad programs with favor, since their existence implies that the institution involved is committed to overseeing the visiting student's experience.

Study-abroad experiences vary widely by type of student, participants' purposes and destinations, and the nature of studies undertaken. Such programs serve students' pragmatic interests, combining travel with a recognized, legitimate form of study likely to count toward a degree. Thus, a European or Asian sojourn need not postpone entry into the labor market (Burn, Cerych, and Smith 1990).

American participants in a study-abroad program listed as their predominant motivations the desire to travel, to experience a new culture, to improve their skills in a foreign language, to gain another perspective on American life, and to obtain a deeper understanding of their host countries. Students expressed hope that the experience would prove useful in their careers, but did not emphasize the importance of the experience as a means of improving career prospects (Carlson, Burn, Useem, and Yachimowicz 1990).

Study abroad also serves the mission of individual institutions. For example, Catholic colleges and universities often establish programs in Rome to study a source point of that faith. A Rome-based program organized by the University of Dallas attracts about 80 percent of that Jesuit college's sophomore-level students. Participants learn about their Greco-Roman heritage, then study European history, art and architecture, philosophy, theology, and Italian language (Goodwin and Nacht 1988).

Like students, schools can have pragmatic reasons behind their interest in foreign study. Study abroad sometimes costs less on the administrative level than does keeping students on the home campus. If a significant portion of the student body attends classes in another country, home-campus classrooms and lecture halls can accommodate additional enrollees.

Study-abroad programs also respond to the needs of faculty members, permitting them to travel and engage in contractual arrangements beyond their home campuses (Goodwin and Nacht 1988). Institutions that alone cannot afford to support study-abroad programs often join consortia geared to such arrangements (McLean 1990).

By the year 2000, 10 percent of American college and university undergraduates should have a significant educational experience abroad before completing their studies, urged a National Task Force report on undergraduate education abroad (Burn and Smuckler 1990). That task force was established by NASFA: the Association of International Educators, the Council on International Educational Exchange (CIEE), and the Institute of International Education (IIE).

Why the sudden need for American students to go abroad? One reason given is the loss of America's competitive position in the world. Adherents of this analysis say that because citizens of other countries are learning to live and work in an international environment, they will find and develop markets, exacerbating the declining economic position of the U.S. (Southern Governors Association Advisory Council on International Education 1986). According to this position, study abroad is essential to regain and maintain economic viability.

The task force's goal of 10 percent of students in study-abroad programs echoes a 1992 target set by the European Community, whose members have begun an extensive exchange program to improve the European market from within. EC nations differ sharply from the United States, however, so it is not clear whether the identical goal is simply a political reaction or a carefully reasoned position.

Either way, indications from surveys of entering American freshmen suggest that the U.S. will meet the 10 percent goal. In 1986, 10.4 percent of first-year students indicated that they were likely to study abroad while enrolled in college (Astin et al. 1986). To make that figure concrete, American students and institutions will have to change; in 1988, only two percent of American undergraduates were studying abroad for academic credit (Zikopoulos 1989).

Institutions are responding to student interest in study abroad by offering more program options. During the 1980s, 66 percent of four-year institutions queried in a Higher Education Panel survey of 541 representative institutions said they have increased opportunities for American students to study abroad (Anderson 1988).

Who actually goes abroad for study? By discipline, the highest proportion comes from the liberal arts (18 percent), languages (16.7 percent), social studies (13.7 percent), and business and management (10.9 percent). Least represented are education (4.1 percent), physical and life sciences (3.8 percent), health sciences (1.7 percent), engineering (1.6 percent), and mathematics and computer sciences (1.3 percent) (Zikopoulos 1988).

Participation varies greatly by institution. The San Diego campus of the University of California system has inaugurated a Fifth College in which all students are strongly encouraged to study abroad. On other campuses, organized study abroad is restricted to the few. Some students do not go abroad because they do not see its curricular relevance or they fear a delayed graduation (Carlson et al. 1990). And while many faculty support the theory of foreign study, they are reluctant to have students in their disciplines study in another country. Often, concern about the quality of courses available abroad drives faculty advisors to urge students who do participate in foreign-study programs to take elective courses while in another country. In a Ford Foundation Study Abroad Articulation Project of deterrents to study abroad encountered by American undergraduates at eight institutions, students cited lack of faculty encouragement as an important reason for not participating (Burn 1991).

... students cited lack of faculty encouragement as an important reason for not participating.

Authors in this field emphasize the need to expand not only the numbers, but the kinds of student who do course work in other countries. Enrollees at baccalaureate institutions are most likely to go abroad; community college students are least likely to do so. Many more women (64 percent) than men study abroad in U.S. programs (Zikopoulos 1988).

American skeptics who argue that professional specializations such as engineering, business, or law cannot accommodate foreign sojourns should note that in European programs, 60 percent of participants major in science, engineering, or other professional fields (Carlson et al. 1990). But unlike U.S. students in these professions, European students are prepared to do course work in the language of the host country. Currently, American students must be satisfied with courses offered in English by the home campus—or with host-country language and culture offerings (Burn 1991).

How does study abroad affect students? Researchers seeking to gauge psychological benefits find it difficult to isolate, measure, and trace attitudinal outcomes specifically to a foreign educational experience. Some reports document substantial personal difficulties among participants in foreign-study programs. Cultural and academic dissimilarities, constrained institutional and governmental budgets, and discontinuities between a student's reasons for foreign study and a country's reasons for encouraging such visits contribute to these negative results (Barber, Altbach, and Meyers 1984; Lulat and Altbach 1985).

Other reports say study abroad generates a positive attitude toward world affairs, enhanced knowledge of the world, greater maturity and interpersonal skills, and reluctance to perpetuate cultural stereotypes (Detweiler 1984). Newer research on study abroad employs crosscultural collaborative approaches to include several home and host countries. In a 1990 survey, foreign-study programs offered by 51 institutions in the United Kingdom, France, Germany, and the U.S. were assessed for their organizational arrangements and impact on participating students (Burn, Cerych, and Smith 1990; Opper, Teichler, and Carlson 1990). The authors analyzed a range of programs, gauging their success in achieving their goals and deciding if particular outcomes could be attributed to program features. They also surveyed students before enrolling in study-abroad programs and after completion to measure the impact of study abroad on foreign-language competence, academic performance, knowledge and perception of host and home countries, and career choice.

Both compulsory and voluntary, the programs assessed also varied greatly in number of participants, duration, and degree of linkage to individual disciplines (with American and Swedish institutions typically serving students from many fields). The study found that no specific aspect of an organization was associated with program success or failure. The researchers concluded that study abroad could take many organizational forms and still function successfully.

The chance to learn firsthand about another culture was most frequently cited by students as the reason for enrolling in the programs. Similarly, fewer than 20 percent of programs studied gave a high priority to the academic dimensions of the experience. However, successful programs that emphasized academic objectives also had a high degree of curricular integration and were designed to reduce the time needed for practical matters such as arranging for housing.

In terms of organization, the U.S. models differed from those in other countries in that they had a designated administrator with primary responsibility for study abroad. Other countries more often assigned the task to a faculty member in exchange for a reduced course load.

How organized should study-abroad programs be? American and British program directors suggested that student support was important in reducing insecurity and calming fears about isolation. But German directors said a high degree of organization support encourages passivity and reduces students' chances to master crosscultural situations—a primary goal of those programs.

Should study-abroad programs be reciprocal among nations and institutions? Most programs are characterized by such symmetry; EC member nations strive not only for joint study programs, but for a single course of study. In some cases, both the home and host institution grant degrees upon completion of the program.

More high school students are studying abroad, a trend worth noting by those in higher education. Programs such as Youth for Understanding and American Field Service conduct much of the better research on the impact of this experience. Their surveys use control samples of nonparticipants of the same age, gender, and educational background as the study-abroad sample.

Some researchers want to know how returnees value the changes brought on by participation in an exchange program. In one study, 661 German and American participants were interviewed and answered questionnaires about their homestay experiences abroad, some of which had been as long as one academic year (Bachner and Zeutschel 1990). Both groups indicated that the key reasons for becoming an exchange student were a desire for increased independence, greater foreign-language proficiency, the honor of the role, and an increased sense of uniqueness.

Students experienced more difficulties in areas that had given them concern prior to the exchange. The more positive a student's relationship with the host family and the longer the student's stay in the host country, the more likely a study participant was to feel that the exchange had been successful. Nearly all Germans reported studying and using English upon returning home, but only 71 percent of Americans reported the same experience with German. On the other hand, among the program's early participants, more Americans than Germans sent their own children on exchanges to the former host country. More U.S. respondents than German respondents declared that the exchange experience had a greater impact on their educational and professional directions.

To prime students for the experience abroad, Georgetown University designed an orientation course contrasting the educational systems of the U.S. and modern Europe—the area to which most Georgetown exchange students choose to go. To prepare students for differences in academic culture, the course is modeled on the European approach, in which faculty generally are not available for extended advising, forcing students to find resources on their own. Involvement in the course carries past a student's actual time abroad, concluding with an assigned paper in the senior year in which the student reflects on the foreign-study experience (Cressey 1991).

At Earlham College, students can avail themselves of an alternative called a bridge activity (Jurasek 1991). In advance of their time abroad, students are encouraged to contact a faculty member from whom they will be taking a course in the two terms immediately following their return. Student and teacher collaborate to define an activity to be conducted while abroad that will have an application to that faculty member's course—not a typical classroom-oriented task like supplemental reading, but an inquiry into some aspect of the host country's culture that might not be covered in the course. This routine is not mandatory; Earlham faculty members fear that making it so would transmogrify the experience into a burden.

Students do not always know how much they have learned while studying abroad. To help gauge the breadth of this masked knowledge, the University of Colorado tests international relations majors before and after study abroad to compare their knowledge and attitudes about the host country pre- and post facto (Delaney 1991). This examination groups questions around program goals:

- To increase familiarity with the host country's cultural, historical, economic, and social background (What cultural activities can you participate in that are unavailable in the U.S.?);
- To learn firsthand the issues being debated in the host country (List the five most controversial topics being covered in the news of the host country);
- To be more sensitive to nations' differing political objectives (Name an issue in which your host country opposes the U.S. stance);

- To recognize the ambiguity in international relations (Describe two different positions held by competing political parties on an issue in your host country);
- To be able to converse with citizens of the host country (Describe a concept that is easily expressed in the language of your host country but not in English); and
- To develop critical thinking skills and an ability to reason in the host-country context (Name three assumptions that you held because of your American background that have been challenged by your stay abroad).

This activity involves the faculty in establishing and measuring the degree to which program goals are attained since the questions reflect them, shows students what they have learned, and responds to state legislature requests to identify the outcomes of study-abroad programs.

Since most American students do not go abroad, what can be done for them? Those who stay at home might encounter students and teachers from other countries, but the experience is not always positive. In the U.S., engineering and computer sciences programs enroll the greatest number of foreign students but send the smallest proportion of American students abroad. In addition, these programs are not designed to take advantage of the way in which foreign students could enhance the international knowledge of their American counterparts. In fact, the limited English of many foreign-born teaching assistants at American institutions might be a significant factor in American students' sometimes negative attitudes about people from other countries.

What can be done to prepare for and build on study-abroad experiences? Institutions trying to increase the quality and participation in study-abroad experiences are finding new ways to inform students about such opportunities and trying to use the expertise of returning participants. However, much remains to be done in this regard; one study of eight American institutions found that only half of foreign-study participants had been told about this option before enrolling in the institution. Kalamazoo College in Michigan was the exception; most students at that institution reported knowing about and participating in study-abroad programs. Among students who did learn in advance of foreign-study options, most said the information in question was general and not related to a particular major (Carlson et al. 1990).

At institutions such as Brown University in Providence, R.I., non-language-department seminars offered in languages other than English challenge students returning from abroad to use their improved foreign-language skills. But few disciplines require fluency in a foreign language at a level needed to participate in a college-level class, so these courses are the exception rather than the rule.

On other campuses, students and faculty are encouraged to discuss the ways in which translation affects the understanding of concepts. This exercise does not require familiarity with another language but provides an opportunity to illustrate how languages reflect cultural differences.

Faculty Development

Any serious curriculum revision requires faculty support; to encourage that involvement in adjusting international dimensions of curricula, American institutions use numerous strategies (McCarthy 1986). These include aiding faculty members in studying abroad themselves as a means of enhancing international awareness and language competence. Undergraduate liberal arts institutions such as Goucher, Earlham, Kalamazoo, and Dickinson have created specific programs to this end.

Campuses with existing programs in other countries use those programs to help faculty improve their language skills. Dickinson sent much of its faculty to partner universities in Spain, France, Germany, and Italy for language study (National Endowment for the Humanities 1984). Government-funded faculty-exchange mechanisms such as the Fulbright Program figure significantly in assisting faculty to gain international experience.

On some campuses, recent immigrants as well as foreign students provide the impetus for investing in faculty study abroad. Although Texas A&I University in Kingsville enrolled many Mexican-American students, most faculty members lacked a sufficient familiarity with this student population's language, culture, and learning styles. To compensate, the university offered faculty members the chance to participate in interdisciplinary seminars on Mexican-American history, culture, and language, as well as annual symposia on Mexican-American issues and a three-week Spanish-immersion summer program in Mexico (FIPSE 1990).

Most institutions do not reward faculty members for participating in activities related to foreign study or for working with foreign students. For example, few campuses attach much value to advising students about study abroad, participating in on-campus activities related to international issues, or serving as a program director in another country; sometimes the trip itself is perceived as sufficient reward (Burn 1991). Faculty members who do not travel abroad in connection with an institutional program sometimes resent those who do. To get more teachers involved in international activities, reward systems on most campuses must change.

Foreign Students

Aware that graduates will be working in multicultural if not international settings, many institutions now acknowledge that their students need opportunities to interact positively with people of other countries and cultures. Therefore, foreign and American students who can teach languages other than English are valuable resources for U.S. colleges and universities, which are finding ways to enlist the help of such individuals. On some campuses, foreign students can register for translation internships or are paid to provide conversation practice in foreign-language courses (Henderson 1983; Laroche 1985). At Ramapo College in Mahwah, N.J., foreign students help translate live satellite transmissions in several languages for course use. Stanford University has a program in which Hispanic students teach Spanish to English-speaking peers (Hubner, Bartolome, Avelar-Lasalle, and Azevedo 1989). At institutions in which no faculty member has a specific language expertise, language mentors from the local community assist students under the supervision of faculty on campus (Marshall 1987).

American institutions enroll foreign students out of the same meld of idealism and pragmatism underlying arguments for sending Americans abroad to study. Foreign students are expected to contribute to the intellectual strength and international perspective of American campuses, enhance institutional income, and become globally inclined individuals who will increase the prospects for world peace (Jenkins 1983).

However, the extent to which these goals are being met has not been measurably demonstrated. Until the 1960s, research on Americans studying abroad and foreign students in the U.S. reflected a post-World War II view of foreign study as an individual crosscultural experience (Barber, Altbach, and Meyers 1984). When federal funds for international education became tied to foreign policy regarding Third World nations, research tended to evaluate the impact of foreign education on economic conditions in sending countries.

For many industrialized countries, foreign graduate students provide much-needed human resources in advanced scientific and technical fields, simultaneously causing a "brain drain" in sending countries. Of Britain's complement of graduate students in engineering and technology, nearly 66 percent are from other countries. In France, foreign graduate students outnumber French nationals two to one. At some institutions in Japan, foreigners constitute nearly half the science and engineering enrollment (Chandler 1989).

Other nations' policies on foreign students influence U.S. decisions to admit foreign students. In 1990, more than 400,000 students from other countries were studying at American educational institutions, making the U.S. the largest receiving country. It hosted nearly one-third of the almost 1,130,000 students who studied abroad around the world in 1988 (Zikopoulos 1991). However, these numbers will not remain static as other nations revise their stances. Foreign-student enrollments continue to increase in the U.S., but the rate is modest when compared with the growth of other leading host countries.

The traditional goals of American exchange programs in bringing students and teachers to the U.S. are to foster mutual understanding; to build cooperative international networks of individuals and institutions; to strengthen Americans' understanding of other regions and nations of the world; to aid developing nations; and to encourage current and future leaders' understanding of U.S. values and culture through direct exposure to U.S. institutions (Liaison Group for International Educational Exchange 1989). But immigration rules, not educational policy, regulate the number of foreign students and teachers on American college and university campuses.

Next to the U.S., France accepts the largest number of foreign students, completely subsidizing the 125,000 who study each year in that country. All students, foreign and domestic, have equal rights and identical requirements for university admission and achievement. As in the U.S., universities in France have the final authority to make decisions regarding enrollment (Chandler 1989; Zikopoulos 1991).

Two approaches to foreign-student policy are emerging in France. The more traditional view is to offer courses to students from North Africa, Europe, and the Middle East who share a common language to help them return and work in their native lands.

French advanced engineering, technical, scientific, and management schools endorse a second approach, seeking ties with industrialized countries, particularly in the European Community. Their objective is to help students learn how to conduct scientific and technical research and to engage in multinational and international endeavors. Nearly 70 percent of the foreign students in these *grandes ecoles* come from North and South America and Europe; only 30 percent are from Africa, Asia, or the Middle East.

In 1989, Germany received 77,445 foreign students—most of whom received government subsidies. That country also runs a competitive scholarship program through the German Academic Exchange Program (DAAD). Applications from abroad for study in Germany generally declined in the late 1980s, despite impressive exchange scholarships and a reputation for high-quality science programs. Lack of familiarity with the German language and educational system might explain this decline. The impact on foreign-student enrollment of German reunification is not yet clear.

France and Germany underwrite the cost of higher education for all students, but Britain—the next largest receiver of foreign students—has a different approach. In 1979, the U.K. began subsidizing only a small proportion of foreign students and began trying to recruit those willing to pay their own way. These efforts have increased the overall numbers of foreign students in Britain; not surprisingly, fewer students from developing countries are coming to the U.K. Services for foreign students, now considered Britain's future trading partners and diplomatic allies, have improved markedly.

Traditionally a society averse to other cultural groups, Japan now has a national commitment to international education. A reform agenda begun in the 1980s encourages Japanese to study abroad; during 1984-89 the number of Japanese students doing so rose 291 percent, and many came to the U.S.

Japan also is working to recruit foreign students; a government target of enrolling 100,000 foreign students in Japanese institutions by 2000 is likely to be met (Ebuchi 1991). Reaching that goal would make Japan the third-largest receiving nation for foreign students. Most foreign students traveling to Japan come from other Asian countries. Echoing programs in Egypt, India, and Australia, Japan is carving a large niche as a new nonwestern destination for foreign students.

Japanese education is opening up in other ways. For example, Japan now permits foreigners to hold university tenure-track positions (Chandler 1989; Kitamura 1983; Mashiko 1989). However, efforts to internationalize Japanese campuses run afoul of scarce housing, cumbersome financial aid rules, an academic year that begins in April rather than September, language barriers, and the perceived low quality of some academic programs.

Throughout the 1980s, Australia debated and changed its foreign-student policy; like Britain, that country moved from subsidizing foreign students to requiring that most pay their fees in full. Debate intensified when institutions short on space for Australian students began admitting more foreign students, and domestic minorities redoubled their demands that Australia erase cultural and language barriers that keep them from receiving a higher education.

Australia's gradual elimination of subsidies for foreign students heightens competition among universities there for foreign students and the income they bring—in 1989, that sum exceeded $300 million in U.S. sums. Even with a sharpened tuition policy, Australian higher education is a relative bargain for Asian students interested in high-quality undergraduate programs in English but unable to afford to travel to Britain, Canada, or the U.S.

Canada is the only major receiving nation that saw foreign-student enrollments decline consistently during the 1980s. Because its overseas students come primarily from a few states—Hong Kong, the U.S., the People's Republic of China, Malaysia, and Singapore—Canada is especially vulnerable to enrollment shifts resulting from economic conditions and foreign-policy decisions. Some Canadians voice alarm at the heavy concentration of Asian foreign students, fearful that many will remain and apply for immigrant status. At the end of the 1980s, Canada increased recruitment, provided more training for students from developing countries, and relaxed immigration requirements regarding student work on campus (Chandler 1989).

Coordinating Educational Mobility
Through International Organizations

International organizations are helping to provide the administrative structure as more students and teachers move from one country to another. The EC hinges its economic survival on the integration of higher education across national borders and so employs transnational mechanisms to coordinate and support study abroad (Luttikholt 1987).

Of four EC activities that bear scrutiny, two deal with study abroad: the European Community Action Scheme for the Mobility of University Students (ERASMUS), a program for university students within the EC; and the Trans-European Mobility Scheme for University Studies (TEMPUS), which extends the ERASMUS program to non-EC nations.

The other EC programs administer credit transfers for students completing course work in another country. The European Community Course Credit Transfer System (ECTS) establishes transnational credit equivalencies within the EC. The Trans-Regional Academic Mobility and Credential Evaluation (TRACE) project extends credit equivalency evaluation beyond the EC.

The EC promotes the "Europeanization" of its higher education and research efforts. ERASMUS, housed in the European Institute for Education and Social Policy, has several goals:

- To promote cooperation among universities in member states;
- To enable 10 percent of students to acquire training in another member state by 1992;
- To increase the mobility of university faculty;
- To strengthen citizen interaction; and
- To provide direct experience in intra-EC cooperation.

To receive ERASMUS grants, institutions must establish contacts with teaching staffs abroad, be prepared to reorganize their curricula and to receive foreign students, and meet their foreign-language instruction needs.

TEMPUS extends ERASMUS to other Western European countries (Austria, Finland, Iceland, Norway, Sweden, and Switzerland), Eastern European countries (Poland, Hungary, Czechoslovakia, Romania, and Bulgaria), and other Organization for Economic Cooperation & Development (OECD)

The EC hinges its economic survival on the integration of higher education across national borders. . . .

members (Australia, Canada, Japan, New Zealand, and the U.S.).

TEMPUS projects require participation with at least one Central European university and two postsecondary institutions in EC nations. The U.S. Education Department Fund for the Improvement of Postsecondary Education (FIPSE) offers grants to American colleges and universities for projects fitting TEMPUS guidelines.

As part of efforts to bolster educational cooperation, the EC endorsed the ECTS, a pilot project that enables students to receive credit for studies they complete in one country from an institution of higher education in another EC country. Variations in standards and regulations are worked out by establishing credit equivalencies among existing courses. Standardized academic transcripts report academic performance. Begun in 1987, the six-year experimental and voluntary program includes business administration, history, medicine, chemistry, and mechanical engineering.

Along with computer advances, EC progress in standardizing reporting of educational credentials has encouraged support for project TRACE. Formally established in 1989, TRACE is creating a decentralized worldwide data network providing information by computer to local, national, regional, and international organizations interested in academic mobility, credential evaluation, and recognition of degrees and diplomas.

TEMPUS will store continuously updated information in English on higher education institutions and systems, as well as credentials granted by higher education institutions.

TRACE is coordinated by the International Association of Universities (IAU) in Paris and supported by representatives from 23 countries and 12 international and nongovernmental organizations. American contributions to TRACE are being led by the National Liaison Committee on Foreign Student Admission of the United States, composed of representatives from the Council for Graduate Schools, College Board, Institute of International Education, American Association of Collegiate Registrars and Admissions Officers, and NAFSA.

To accomplish these massive exchange projects, students and faculty must become multilingual. Many EC countries are reevaluating their language policies. The Netherlands boasts one of the world's most successful and comprehensive foreign-language programs, requiring grammar-school students to take three languages for at least four years.

But political and economic change continues to boost demand for multilingual competence, and Dutch policy makers now say all language needs cannot be met within its formal education system, which is limited to English, French, German, and Spanish at the secondary level.

To improve EC-wide language instruction, a Brussels-based program called Lingua supports initial and inservice training for language teachers, language learning programs in vocational and higher education, and exchanges between young people in professional, vocational, and technical education, limiting languages covered to those of the EC: Danish, Dutch, English, French, German, Greek, Irish, Italian, Luxembourgish, Portuguese, and Spanish.

The EC's position with regard to language competency is that every member state should provide a practical competence in two foreign languages for pupils in compulsory education. At least one of these should be the national language of another member state (Van Els 1988).

The EC promotes university-industry cooperation and has endorsed a program titled Action Programme of the Community in Education and Training for Technology (COMETT), which coordinates such projects. COMETT will develop a European network of University-Enterprise Training Partnerships; create exchanges of students and personnel between universities and industry; develop and test joint university-enterprise projects in continuing education; support multilateral initiatives for developing multimedia training systems; and monitor and evaluate the projects (Luttikholt 1987).

A long-standing UNESCO project encourages countries to establish mechanisms for recognizing degrees and diplomas worldwide and for establishing equivalencies among them. Like many other countries, Canada is creating a National Commission for the Recognition of Studies, Degrees, and Diplomas as part of a larger effort to coordinate and standardize degree and diploma evaluations. A Canadian commission will facilitate the implementation of the UNESCO Convention on the Recognition of Studies, Degrees, and Diplomas. That body will work to make Canadian degrees and diplomas better known overseas and promote their recognition in other countries (*IAU Bulletin* June 1990).

Summary and Research Needed
On Educational Mobility

American strengths

For many years, American colleges and universities have used the credit-transfer system to permit some students to complete portions of their studies in other countries; some institutions have encouraged students to do so. Since most students were paying for the foreign-study experience, decisions about going abroad tended to take on a pragmatic cast, with foreign study usually elected by students majoring in foreign languages, art, history, and other fields militating in favor of career-oriented interest in international affairs.

Institutions sending students abroad developed long-term relationships with colleges and universities in other countries—a pattern that is being replicated as a new generation of colleges and universities move into the field. Surveys indicate that more American students plan to study in another country, prompting more institutions to make arrangements in that regard. Some institutions are trying to integrate study abroad into major fields of study, with a comparably valuable crosscultural experience sometimes offered for students who cannot or do not want to travel abroad.

Coupled with relatively mild U.S. controls on foreign-student entry and exit, U.S. institutions' ability to convey specialized expertise in fields sought after by people from other countries have drawn many of the best foreign students to American campuses. These students offer Americans an opportunity to communicate with and learn to understand other cultures.

American weaknesses

Despite the long history of Americans studying abroad, lapses in continuity exist between the foreign and domestic educational experiences of students. Courses taken by Americans abroad often are considered peripheral to their majors; when these students return to the U.S., they rarely are asked to extrapolate from their foreign experiences to enrich the home campus.

More American students are going abroad, but many still do not have this chance. When specialized expertise was the motivating force behind an academic sojourn in another country, the limited numbers of study-abroad participants seemed appropriate. But as more institutions encourage students to seek international experience *qua* international experience, American study-abroad program scope and participation seems inadequate, if not parochial. For example, the list of countries to which American students and faculty can go is curbed sharply by prospective participants' inability to speak languages other than English. Additionally, many Americans lack basic understanding about the country in which they want to study.

Institutions often lack concrete policies on foreign-student admissions, such as the desired number of foreign students, acceptance criteria, tuition, numbers, scholarships, and services. Sometimes foreign students are viewed as drains on the enrolling institution; research suggests that many are dissatisfied with the education they receive. This aspect of American international education might be forced to change as competition increases for the best and brightest foreign students and as American administrators compare their attitudes with those in other countries, which see foreign students as valued guests.

Most schools have not integrated programs to help faculty improve language skills, provide an international dimension to their courses, or go abroad themselves. Faculty retain parochial attitudes toward the educational benefit of study in another country and are slow to erase scheduling conflicts and requirements that bar many students from studying abroad.

At the international level, although the U.S. belongs to networks of international organizations that provide an administrative structure for student mobility, the European Community provides leadership in this area.

Research needed
With studies of attitude change constituting much of the research in this field, such inquiries should consider links between students' academic preparation (including language fluency), location and duration of study abroad or internship experience, and the main body of a student's academic program. How much time is needed to gain a useful understanding of another culture? Could experiences obtained in the U.S. be as beneficial as those obtained abroad?

Assessment of Americans who study abroad generally deals with different issues than does research on foreign students in the U.S. However, in matters of common challenge such as acculturation or crosscultural communication, the results of comparative studies would be interesting. Research in both directions is needed to add an international perspective for crosscultural research. Are there additional ways such inquiries could improve the international education of Americans who do not go abroad?

National

The federal role in movements of students from one country raises questions. Should the U.S. set policy on recruitment and admission of foreign students, or are existing immigration regulations and supply and demand factors sufficient? Is there a need for a federally funded or mandated clearinghouse or similar mechanism to facilitate international student and faculty exchange? Where have foreign students who studied in the U.S. gone after graduation, and what are the implications of that data for American foreign policy?

International

Can multinational exchanges that benefit the U.S. and other countries be organized through international bodies? Given the number of Americans who study abroad and the number of foreign students who come to the U.S., what are the advantages to the U.S. in joining European Community exchange networks? Should the U.S. join regional exchange networks for the Americas and Canada or the Pacific Basin countries?

For many people, international education deals with study abroad, foreign-student affairs, or curriculum dealing with international issues—but not all three and rarely in concert. International education on American campuses often consists of a collection of discrete activities with no comprehensive structure. Administrators who manage programs that send American students to study elsewhere in the world might have little knowledge of foreign students enrolling in their institutions or of faculty exchanges, development contracts, or programs for non-English-speaking American students.

International Program Models in the U.S.

Since World War II, evolving international relationships and national educational systems have spawned new laws and regulations regarding education and training of people from other countries. Institutions have added more administrators to carry out increasing numbers of bilateral, multinational, and international education agreements. Buffeted by a changing world economy and worldwide tumult in foreign policy, these offices operate within volatile—and now shrinking— budgets. Aside from anecdotal information suggesting that early experiences living in another culture are a factor, little information exists about the paths that lead administrators into careers in international program management.

In the 1990s, administrators serve many constituencies. Domestic responsibilities include foreign-student advisement and credentials evaluation, study-abroad coordination and exchange agreements, English and foreign-language proficiency testing, English and foreign-language teaching, international visitor briefing, support services and counseling for foreign and American students, international grants and contract oversight, and liaisons with local, state, national, and international associations.

On the international side, administrators manage overseas programs and projects, provide consulting and translation services, and direct community and government relations activities. The American group's professional voice is the Association of International Education Administrators (AIEA), formed in 1982. Through a journal, *International Education Forum and Newsletter*, AIEA provides information exchange and a network for individuals interested in international studies and services. An AIEA-published pamphlet, *Guidelines to International Education at U.S. Colleges and Universities,* offers suggestions on international program administration.

Gauging the frequency of these activities at two- and four-year American institutions, researchers have found that the most common task of international education administrators is to provide foreign-student services. After the foreign-student advisor, four-year institutions are most likely to designate an administrator to coordinate study-abroad programs; two-year institutions hire administrators to coordinate foreign-language instruction (Anderson 1988).

Some advocates urge that comprehensive international education works best when all elements are coordinated by a center on campus, sometimes called an Office of International Programs (American Council on Education 1984; Backman 1984; Harari 1983). In general, institutions pay greater heed to internal bureaucracies that have office space, large budgets, and directors with seniority in the hiring system. Coordination is said to strengthen individual programs, enhance interaction among program participants, and heighten the on-campus visibility of international programs. The roles of these offices vary by institutional size and type. Responsibilities include:

1. Supporting efforts to internationalize the curriculum;
2. Acting as a liaison to other units within the institution that administer international activities;
3. Administering study-abroad programs;
4. Administering international (foreign) student programs;
5. Promoting student, faculty, and staff exchange programs and other incentives for engaging in international education activities;
6. Negotiating and implementing contracts and grants with foreign universities, governments, and businesses;
7. Cooperating with international interests in the community, including citizenship-education programs and business activities;
8. Supporting regional, national, and international associations and consortia;
9. Preparing proposals to foreign agencies, foundations, business, and other entities to help implement the institution's international commitment; and
10. Interpreting national and international trends and opportunities and providing leadership for the institution (Harari 1983).

Administrators who direct these units recommend a central bureaucracy, but no research demonstrates a relation between type of administrative structure and quality of education received by participating students. However, institutional type and size are good predictors of organizational structure. Reflecting the tendency of American colleges and universities to support unique goals and missions, most books describe international program offices at individual institution levels. Backman (1984) describes in detail how 17 American institutions deliver international education, discerning among state universities, private colleges and universities, and community colleges. Written mostly by directors of international-education programs, these case studies begin with brief histories of the origins and development of international-educational activities at the institution. Then, missions and goals are discussed with respect to international education, international unit administrative organization, program components, funding, program strengths and weaknesses, and future plans.

Internationalization Indexes

Few question whether a campus can be "too international," but in light of increased competition for status and funds to support international activities, it is logical to wonder whether one campus can be "more international" than another. Some articles rank U.S. campuses on a continuum ranging from those evincing little interest in international offerings to those displaying a great deal of interest. One of the first such continuums was constructed by the American Association of State Colleges and Universities from results of a 1981 survey of member institutions. The exercise separated institutions into five levels of "internationalization."

The one extreme consisted of colleges and universities reporting no visible international curriculum activity, listing mostly western-oriented courses, enrolling a small percentage of the student body in study-abroad experiences, and describing no plans for involvement in international education. The other pole was occupied by institutions reporting majors with specific international foci, heavy enrollment in study-abroad programs, substantial numbers of foreign students and services for those students, large numbers of faculty studying or working abroad, some foreign faculty and visitors on campus, a record of development contracts in other countries, and an office of international programs (Harari 1983).

An index developed by Henson, Noel, Gillard-Byers, and Ingle (1990) considered a combination of quantitative and qualitative factors in scoring institutional internationalism. (Quantitative measures: type and level of activities engaged in by faculty and departments; foreign-language requirements; enrollments in internationally oriented courses; funds available for international activities and private-sector expectations. Qualitative measures: priority commitment from administrators; institutional plans indicating attention to this topic; faculty competence in international affairs).

Afonso (1990) used exclusively quantitative measures appropriate for land-grant institutions to develop an International Dimension Index (IDI) instrument using 14 measures, including foreign languages (number of foreign languages, enrollments, and degrees offered in them), area/ethnic studies (number of degrees conferred), foreign-student enrollment, membership in NAFSA, faculty awards for foreign teaching or research (number of Fulbright awards), foreign faculty on campus (number of foreign Fulbright recipients hosted), and funding levels for international projects (Title VI area center and grant awards and National Science Foundation research with international implications). Smaller, teaching-oriented institutions might be more interested in different measures such as proportion of students at advanced foreign-language levels or proportion of courses offered with a foreign-language component.

Evaluating campuswide international efforts remains an important goal; in the absence of such measures, generalizations and trends cannot be discussed and improvements cannot be made. Multiple indexes probably will grow out of the widely differing goals of American institutions for international education.

Using Consortia to Carry Out International Education

Colleges and universities in the U.S. often use cooperative consortia arrangements to ease administrative burdens and stretch resources for international activities, especially in straitened economic times. In 1987, four-year institutions in the U.S. reported participating in consortia primarily to conduct study-abroad programs, offer foreign-language instruction in less commonly taught languages, and teach specialized international-studies courses (Anderson 1988).

Consortium participation often permits institutions to offer more international topics. In a localized project, the Russian Studies department at the University of Minnesota and the Program of Russian Area Studies of the five Associated Colleges of the Twin Cities (Augsburg College, Hamline University, Macalester College, the College of Saint Catherine, and the College of Saint Thomas) established a cooperative program to improve undergraduate Russian language and area-studies courses (Title VI 1987-88).

Some consortia pool resources statewide. The Pennsylvania Council for International Education (PaCIE) brings together faculty members and administrators to discuss programs and provides follow-up campus consultation visits by experts who suggest avenues to program improvement (Dinniman and Burkart 1988). The Virginia Tidewater Consortium for Higher Education, in cooperation with the Public Broadcasting System, offers television news broadcasts in French and Spanish to member institutions and the public. Other consortia are regional; for example, the Great Lakes Colleges Association (GLCA) and the Associated Colleges of the Midwest (ACM) number among their activities management of overseas-study programs for member schools.

Institutions also join consortia to heighten their visibility and improve chances for program and research funding.

Institutions also join consortia to heighten their visibility and improve chances for program and research funding. To document contributions by their graduates to international affairs, a group of liberal arts colleges created a consortium called the International 50, publicizing data showing that students from these institutions tend to pursue international careers (Engerman and Marden 1992). Many joined the Peace Corps, went on to be foreign-service officers and even ambassadors, or worked in multinational corporations. The consortia's efforts helped liberal arts colleges, which enroll only a fraction of the students in higher education, to highlight the effectiveness of their work.

Consortia seem highly successful in helping institutions with limited resources widen opportunities in international education, but systematic testing is needed to uncover the reasons why some can overcome institutional rivalries and faculty jealousies and others cannot (Lambert 1980).

Strategies for Promoting International Education On Campus

Many colleges and universities want to revise their international-education programs. Before making changes, however, an institution must know what it already is doing. A 1981 Council on Learning worksheet for program planning and evaluation of international studies and foreign languages suggested collecting data in the following areas:

- Curriculum: organization of international, area, and foreign-language studies; institutional requirements;
- Budget, funding and grants;
- Cooperative efforts with other institutions;
- Faculty involvement: exchanges, foreign visitors, curriculum workshops;
- Student life and extracurricular activities: study-abroad programs, student clubs, international speakers;
- Learning resources: language laboratories, library collections; and
- Enrollments in internationally oriented courses.

A more complete listing of current international educational activities on campuses today would include:

- Research and development projects and other agreements with organizations abroad;
- International majors and minors for foreign as well as American students;
- Centralized international-affairs offices or administrative networks to carry out international activities;
- Materials support for international activities including international satellite telecommunications, computer network capability, and use of videodisc and other high-technology teaching tools in internationally focused courses;
- Cooperative work projects run in conjunction with study abroad;
- Outreach to elementary and secondary schools and the community; and
- Involvement in state, national, and international organizations, consortia, foundations, and businesses that deal with international education.

These missing areas indicate where administrative changes in higher education institutions have occurred since the 1980s.

Actual change depends on institution type, faculty expertise, geographical location, and a college's or university's historical experience in the field of international education. Between 1982 and 1987, four-year American institutions reported increased foreign-student enrollment and more opportunities for U.S. students and faculty to study abroad. More than half had increased the number of international course offerings, hired new faculty with international expertise, and added to the international collection in their libraries. During the same period, two-year institutions reported fewer changes, but one in six noted increased integration of international materials into regular courses and in foreign-student enrollments (Anderson 1988).

What strategies do administrators say they are using to put an international dimension on their campuses? A survey of administrators at the level of dean and above at American universities (Henson et al. 1990) found the top five priorities for international activities on campus to be the following:

1. Establish cooperative relationships with institutions in other countries;
2. Offer study- or internships-abroad opportunities for U.S. students;
3. Encourage foreign-language study;
4. Recruit and train foreign students; and
5. Include more international content in the curriculum.

These findings agree with results of an American Council on Education survey of some 400 two-year institutions as well as four-year colleges and universities. Participants reported an astonishing 44 percent increase in contacts with foreign institutions among the nation's four-year colleges (Anderson 1988).

Asked how they would use additional funds for international education, four-year institutions said they would develop new internationally oriented courses, expand study-abroad opportunities, hire faculty with international expertise, and provide support for faculty to work abroad. Two-year institutions responded in similar fashion but in a different order. They want to hire faculty with international expertise, deepen their libraries' international collections, develop internationally oriented courses, and expand study-abroad opportunities.

Many people believe that lack of funding is an impassable barrier to implementing international-education efforts. The ACE study reports that at American four-year institutions, funds come most frequently from private foundations, individual donors, and the U.S. Department of Education. Institutions also receive support from the National Endowment for the Humanities, state governments, business firms, and the Department of State/USIA.

Comprehensive collections of funding sources appear in Harari (1983), Hoopes (1984), the *International Studies Funding and Resources Book* (Council on International and Public Affairs 1990), and *Financial Resources for International Study* (1989). However, although budget is important, it does not always determine the degree to which an institution supports international-educational activities. The wittily titled *Without a Nickel* (Leinwald 1983) describes ways in which colleges and universities support international education without significant financial outlay.

Some campuses take an integrated approach to planning for international-educational activities, including the president, chancellor, board of trustees, supporting corporations, and alumni into the process. At some institutions, trustees have an international committee that considers where to direct the vice president for development to ask for funds for international initiatives and continuing programs. At others, alumni living abroad are asked for advice and support. At many institutions, corporate heads and state commerce department members serve on advisory councils that inform the institution of state employment needs.

Crossinstitutional task forces can gather background data on institutional strengths and needs, including existing funded projects, student population composition, local branches of multinational corporations, international programs, and enrollments in them. Using these data, an institution's president can incorporate international objectives into a strategic plan and set priorities for achieving them. Institutional accountability requires documentation of progress toward achievement of goals, and progress reports are integral to planning. When international goals are incorporated into general institutional planning, they are less likely to be omitted from future plans or budgets.

U.S. Programs in Other Countries

As more American institutions begin to operate programs outside the U.S., American administrators are asking how these programs should be administered and regulated. The Commission on Postsecondary Accreditation (COPA) accredits foreign components of American institutions and some foreign institutions by using a 10-point assessment program (Commission On Postsecondary Accreditation 1987) that asks whether institutions are:

- Military education programs on overseas installations, offered under the aegis of United States-based institutions that are under contract with the armed forces;
- U.S.-based institutions with foreign campuses and branches;
- Study-abroad and related academic programs of U.S.institutions;
- Programs jointly delivered by U.S.-domestic accredited institutions and foreign institutions;
- Institutions chartered in the U.S. and historically designed to serve U.S. citizens, but existing physically outside the U.S.;
- Foreign institutions with foreign charters but with no U.S.connection other than accreditation;
- Canadian or other foreign institutions whose accreditation procedures are identical to the U.S.; or
- Foreign institutions affiliated by specific program to accredited domestic institutions.

Programs involving a year or semester abroad generally have well-defined missions and a history of good practice. They provide crosscultural orientation and on-site support for students; programs are evaluated as part of the overall institutional accreditation visit (Mayhew 1990).

Most frequently, programs that do not meet American standards of good practice are joint ventures between specific programs of American institutions and foreign institutions. Sometimes problems arise because a venture's goal is not clearly stated; sometimes the difficulty is that the program is being run for profit rather than education (Mayhew 1990). Chambers and Cummings (1990) discuss contractual issues related to agreements between American and Japanese institutions in which joint ventures have increased dramatically.

Professional associations respond to reports of abuse by issuing guidelines for American programs in other countries. A statement of good practice for overseas international education programs for non-U.S. nationals by the Middle States Commission on Higher Education (1989) suggests steps to take in regard to clarifying institutional mission, governing board authorization, instructional programs, resources, admissions and record keeping, student support, control and administration, ethics and public disclosure, and contractual arrangements with other parties.

International Attempts at Self-Regulation

American methods of self-regulation and self-recognition are spreading as institutions worldwide gain autonomy. In 1988, two private associations of educational institutions, the Commission on Higher Education of the Middle States Association (CHE/MSA) and the Dominican Association for Self-Study and Accreditation (Asociacion Dominicana Para El Autoestudio Y La Acreditacion (ADAA), agreed to collaborate on training workshops in self-study and accreditation procedures, supervision visits, and other activities (Middle States Association 1988).

How should education be regulated outside a country's borders when programs are no longer arrangements between individual institutions or bilateral agreements among governments, but multilateral agreements administered by international organizations? With a burgeoning international-education industry extending beyond existing national laws but not yet under international agreements, governments are tightening controls on higher education programs operated by foreign institutions, imposing new laws and more domestic taxes. Stein (1990) discusses tax implications resulting from the British Education Reform Act of 1988 and outlines legal issues for American institutions with programs in England.

For tax purposes, Britain distinguishes between programs sponsored by foreign institutions and conducted in Britain and British organizations that accept and teach foreign students as part of the regular course of studies or in a separate curriculum specifically designed for them. These new policies have implications for accreditation, institutional and individual income taxes, tax transfers, and value-added taxes.

American institutions often want to establish exchange agreements with institutions abroad, but many do not know where to begin. In 1984, the American Council on Education issued guidelines regarding academic exchange of students and faculty members to help institutions seeking exchange partners. That pamphlet lists contacts at 23 American organizations and Fulbright Commissions in 42 countries capable of assisting a U.S. institution in finding a partner for exchange. A newer report from ACE lists Central and Eastern European universities seeking cooperative arrangements with American institutions; this publication lists institutions in Czechoslovakia, Hungary, Poland, Romania, the Commonwealth of Independent Republics (formerly the U.S.S.R.), and Yugoslavia (November 1990).

An Institute of International Education Report describes changes in international educational exchange in these countries as of 1989. Language barriers persist as do difficulties resulting from differences in educational systems and the reorganization of the economies of these countries. Despite these obstacles, American students and scholars going to East Central European countries found the experience a rewarding one. In return, these countries are now eager for academic exchanges (Burn n.d.).

International Administrative Arrangements

Colleges and universities tend to think of international education occurring on a campus through a curriculum's international and comparative orientation—or through student exchanges and other cooperative agreements of colleges and universities that cross national boundaries. However, international education also can take place as a result of bilateral or multilateral government agreements. Projects supported by private and public international organizations can encourage the process, and an international element can be delivered through distance-learning approaches that transcend national boundaries with new computer and satellite technologies.

Many new agreements are multilateral and multilevel. For example, an important function of international organizations is to facilitate cross-border access to information—a role enhanced by the expansion of electronic networks and computerized databases. In a project directly affecting American researchers, the International Association of Universities (IAU) has agreements with two regional divisions of UNESCO and the U.S.-funded ERIC Clearinghouse on Higher Education to create a common English/French thesaurus for indexing educational documents. This will permit retrieval of ERIC databases through the UNESCO system, allowing international access to American educational research. Efforts on the American side to access the UNESCO database also are under way.

Among the impressive sorts of administrative arrangements than can cross national boundaries is a set of administrative structures begun by the European Community. In the past 20 years, the EC has moved dramatically toward unifying its educational systems in anticipation of 1992 and the establishment of a true European common market. Projects approved include programs encouraging student and teacher exchanges, promoting foreign-language instruction, exploring technology links for distance education, funding university-industry partnerships, and exploring the possibility of a European educational satellite system.

In administrative matters, the U.S. and other countries are beginning to talk with each another. To improve the integration of various higher educational systems, Western Europe is working toward an academic course-credit system akin to that of U.S. higher education. At the same time, many American institutions should be aiming to develop an EC-style study-abroad model for internationalizing their professional education programs (Carlson et al. 1990).

Summary and Research Needed in Administration

American strengths
At colleges and universities in the U.S., international education derives its form and content from each institution's mission and resources. Administrative structures reflect each institution's programs and commitments, resulting in a wide diversity of successful approaches. Development of such programs has been encouraged by foreign-student demand for American education, American prosperity and technical expertise, and comparatively liberal laws governing flow of people and information across national boundaries.

American weaknesses
In the absence of a national clearinghouse for inquiries from other nations about American education, international contacts at the institutional level are necessary. However, efforts to create links between U.S. institutions and those in other coun-

tries are hindered by language barriers and lack of knowledge of comparative educational systems. Additionally, American administrators often lack a comprehensive view of what international education means for the campus community.

At the international level, American higher education has not used every possible contact with other countries or with national or international organizations—instead, generally opting for institution-to-institution arrangements.

Research needed

At the institutional level, researchers need to analyze the effectiveness of administrative structures above the stratum of the individual program. Such analysis could include investigating the success of alternative administrative arrangements such as consortia.

At the national level, longitudinal career surveys are needed to measure the background and training of international program administrators. Given the changing demands imposed on this role, such study should include critical factors that prompted this choice of career. Consideration also ought to go to the academic preparation needed by someone entering this track, along with evaluations of programs now offering training in the field.

In comparative administration, the literature extensively covers only foreign-student affairs. Few comprehensive data exist on use by other countries of multinational or international bodies to support and extend educational efforts. Subjects especially worthy of study include foreign institutions in the U.S., American institutions outside the U.S., and institutions linked to campuses worldwide via satellite.

International treaties and other agreements on higher education are increasing in number faster than entities and mechanisms with which to implement them are evolving. Researchers would do well to assess which agreements need to be written for cooperation on an international scale and what types of organizations would best serve higher education worldwide.

SUMMARY AND CONCLUSIONS

Americans increasingly are aware that they live, work, and think in a global marketplace—an awareness that propels them to demand more emphasis in educational programs on international topics. The changes that render the nations of the world ever more interdependent require colleges to work harder to produce graduates familiar with other cultures and their histories, languages, and institutions.

People coming out of American higher education must be more cognizant of the ties that bind the regions of the world. They must be willing to consider perspectives held by people whose cultures differ from their own. They also must be competent to conduct education, business, and governmental activities in an international environment and prepared to make personal and public-policy decisions as responsible citizens of an international society.

To meet these and related challenges, colleges and universities in the U.S. are incorporating their goals for international education into campuswide strategic plans and enriching academic disciplines with a comparative and international view. Institutions are revising curricula to alert all students to the languages and cultures of other countries, while creating faculty development opportunities that stress an international outlook.

Some institutions are encouraging students from other countries and American students with international experiences to contribute more actively to the curriculum; others are devising new structures to coordinate burgeoning international activities. Many colleges and universities are joining consortia that bring together academia and businesses and local, national, and international organizations to pursue international interests.

Every discipline and every professional school can be involved in this expanded framework which, for purposes of this volume, includes the study of international relations, area studies, foreign languages and cultures, comparative and international approaches to particular disciplines, and environmental, global, or peace studies.

Higher education takes on international tones when participants come from more than one country or when institutions administer exchange programs, branch campuses, or have other crossnational ties. An increasingly complex network links academic institutions, private groups, businesses, government at many levels, and public and private interna-

People coming out of American higher education must be more cognizant of the ties that bind the regions of the world.

tional organizations.

The first colleges in the U.S. approached international education by teaching foreign languages, comparative linguistics, and area studies (McCaughey 1984). Interest in international studies, political science, and international relations grew after World War I, buoyed by the hope that the world could achieve peace and security if peoples of all nations could learn more about one another.

International student exchanges gained momentum in the 1920s and 1930s but were interrupted by World War II. After peace returned in 1945, the concept of the approved international study-abroad programs gained wide acceptance. Americans began studying abroad in record numbers and more foreign students came to the U.S., prompting the establishment of credentialing systems and bodies to represent the interests of students, administrators, and institutions.

In the 1990s, the emergence of a global economy, increased access to and interest in other parts of the world, and improved electronic communications have combined to spread international topics across the curriculum. The decentralized nature of American higher education lets public and private institutions link up with educators in other countries, revise curricula to meet the career goals of graduates, and create administrative structures to carry out international interchanges that reflect institutional missions.

Curriculum Reform

Once tightly focused on improving the international expertise of language majors and foreign-affairs experts, American colleges and universities have gained interest in teaching all students about other countries and cultures. Institutions are revising general education courses to require exposure to several countries and cultures, broadening history- and civilization-course coverage of nonwestern countries, tightening standards on foreign-language proficiency, and including foreign languages and study or work abroad in professional programs (Lambert 1989). This trend is evident in two-year, four-year, and graduate programs; depth and breadth of curricular applications vary.

Curriculumwide at many campuses, faculty are adding international texture to their courses by stretching syllabi to include books, films, videos, music, and newspapers from other countries. Advanced nonlanguage courses are taught in tongues other than English. Some institutions offer extra-diplomate certification to students who complete a series of internationally focused courses. Others offer double majors or new minors with an international focus. Computer- and satellite-technology advances allow American students to interact directly with counterparts in other countries. Electronic simulations connecting students around the world are especially useful in providing an international experience within the confines of the domestic classroom.

More students are studying abroad, but curriculum planners question whether academic programs sufficiently integrate this experience. A few places award core course credit for work completed abroad (Burn 1991). Some campuses are putting more effort into devising orientation programs for departing students and debriefing programs for students returning from stays abroad. At other institutions, students returning from study abroad may have the option of enrolling in courses requiring advanced language facility. Some programs ask returning foreign-study participants to act as peer advisors in recruitment activities for international-study programs. Foreign students, Americans who have lived abroad, minority students, and internationally seasoned local residents tutor others in foreign languages and crosscultural communication skills.

Some institutions encourage these curricular changes by supporting faculty-development activities. They send faculty to other countries to learn another language, provide language tutors on the home campus, organize summer curriculum-development workshops, engage experts from other institutions to act as consultants, sponsor exchanges, encourage group study tours, offer release time for international projects, and supplement salaries for study, research, and travel abroad. In return, faculty are expected to equip their courses with more content about other countries—possibly incorporating material in languages other than English. Teachers proficient in non-English languages sometimes are encouraged to offer their courses in that alternate language. However, faculty-development programs are still the exception rather than the rule, and few institutions offer programs designed to help academic administrators who are institutional leaders gain an international perspective.

Institutions that factor community outreach into their missions provide intensive foreign-language and international-business courses for local business and civic groups. Many offer inservice programs on international and global issues for elementary and secondary school teachers. To obtain funding and program support, more institutions are asking multinational corporations for financial support and internship spaces in their companies in the U.S. and elsewhere. Faculty members interested in enhancing the international component of their courses can take advantage of the efforts of single-discipline organizations which collect and publish course descriptions with international components (Groennings and Wiley 1990).

It is difficult to construct international measures of knowledge and attitudes about other countries, and few such instruments have been administered in more than one country (Cogan, Torney-Purta, and Anderson 1988). There is little journal coverage of efforts by higher education organizations outside the U.S. to promote the study of other countries—a situation that might improve as a result of international efforts to merge educational databases and increasing interaction among higher education organizations around the world.

Study Abroad and Foreign Students

At colleges and universities worldwide, more students are studying outside their home countries. In European Community countries, student mobility is on the rise. By 1992, ERASMUS aims to see at least 10 percent of EC students acquiring academic training in another member state. That percentage is the same goal being eyed by U.S. institutions, which want to encourage not only an increase in the number of American students enrolling in programs abroad, but a wider array of countries where they may go (Burn and Smuckler 1990).

The U.S. government is taking some fiscal steps to encourage study abroad. The National Security Education Act of 1991 triples federal funding for undergraduate study abroad and directs more money to underwrite graduate research overseas as well as for grant support for programs in international and area studies and foreign languages.

Crossnational analyses of study-abroad programs provide alternative models that institutions can consider in structuring their arrangements (Burn, Cerych, and Smith 1990; Opper, Teichler, and Carlson 1990). The U.S. remains at the top of the list of nations that attract foreign students, but the policies of other nations could exert considerable influence on foreign students' choices in the future (Chandler 1989). For example, Australia and Japan are working harder to attract enrollment in their higher education systems among students from Asian countries who now dominate the foreign enrollment at American institutions.

Administering International Education

International higher education takes place through a world network of organizations that grew during the late 1980s and early 1990s. This growth was spurred by changing relations between higher education and those who employ graduates, organizations supporting student mobility, and advances in computer and telecommunications technology. At the institutional level, these changes have meant increased individual contacts with other countries and more administrators to coordinate the resulting activities. Institutions want to establish cooperative programs in other countries, offer more foreign study and internships, encourage foreign-language study, recruit and train foreign students, and include more international content in the curriculum (Anderson 1988).

The U.S. government modestly funds programs for international education and foreign-language study, business-education ventures, educational development contracts, and exchange programs. State and local governments have moved to coordinate efforts across educational sectors and between education and local business (National Governors Association 1989). Governors are interested in educational quality; they want better measures of student knowledge about other countries. More states are requiring foreign-language entrance and exit requirements for public colleges and universities (Draper 1989).

At the international level, U.S. liaison committees are cooperating with European Community and UNESCO projects to standardize educational credential reporting, licensing, and certification requirements; ease student mobility across national educational systems; and develop compatible databases for information exchange (European Center for Higher Education 1987). The European Community leads the effort to create a comprehensive structure for administering international higher education (Luttikholt 1987).

As higher education follows other industries into the global marketplace, more Americans see schooling as an international commodity. Governments are scrutinizing joint educational business ventures and increasing regulatory controls on them (Chambers and Cummings 1990; Stein 1990).

Promoting an International Perspective

The decentralized nature of American higher education has allowed state systems and private institutions to create links with educators in other countries, revise curricula to meet the job requirements encountered by graduates, and create entities to carry out international interchanges that reflect institutional missions. The latitude they enjoy has kept some colleges and universities from noticing worldwide changes in education. Nationalism and its historical and cultural markers continue to guide individual nations' participation in and response to international education. But as nations expand joint educational endeavors, they influence one another's understanding of the term. Newer research, couched in crossnational and international contexts, can reveal obstacles as well as opportunities implicit in a more international understanding of the concept.

How can individual faculty and administrators encourage development of an international perspective on their campuses? They must clarify the term's meaning on each campus and evaluate institutional policies on international and foreign-language studies, foreign students, and faculty development against that definition. Other elements of this basic appraisal include:

Curriculum reform. Assess the degree to which all students on your campus are exposed to other languages and cultures, and measure the learning that results. Are international elements infused into courses, even at professional schools? Do students acquire the foreign-language proficiency demanded by their career goals? Institutions at least should produce graduates knowledgeable of other peoples and cultures, professionally competent to conduct education, business, and governmental activities at an international level, sensitive to intercultural differences, prepared to extend scientific understanding through collaborative transnational research, and familiar enough with world affairs that they can be responsible citizens of an international community (Hayden 1982).

Read journal articles on how postsecondary institutions abroad provide an international education through their curricular offerings. Attend conferences attracting international audiences. Consider whether your campus might benefit from curriculum projects carried out by multinational and international organizations.

Educational mobility. Widen chances for international contact by sending Americans abroad, bringing foreign students to the U.S., and using international telecommunications in the classroom. Help lengthen the list of potential study sites abroad. Make it possible for students to participate in study-abroad programs by removing the academic and other institutional barriers preventing them from going. Query foreign and American students and faculty with international experience on the countries they know, and enlist them in supporting second-language instruction and crosscultural communication on campus. Encourage organizations and institutions to establish and maintain state and federal programs that increase the number and broaden the types of students who can go abroad, and prepare them to learn from that experience. Evaluate the U.S. role in efforts by international organizations to improve student mobility and consider the implications for your own campus.

Administering international education. Evaluate institutional structures that help and hinder international education activities on campus. Coordinate with other institutions and consortia including community, state, national, and international organizations. Investigate how individual institutions can benefit from educational work by international bodies and the avenues to participation in these efforts.

REFERENCES

The Educational Resources Information Center (ERIC) Clearinghouse on Higher Education abstracts and indexes the current literature on higher education for inclusion in ERIC's data base and announcement in ERIC's monthly bibliographic journal, *Resources in Education* (RIE). Most of these publications are available through the ERIC Document Reproduction Service (EDRS). For publications cited in this bibliography that are available from EDRS, ordering number and price code are included. Readers who wish to order a publication should write to the ERIC Document Reproduction Service, 7420 Fullerton Rd., Suite 110, Springfield, VA 22153-2852. (Phone orders with VISA or MasterCard are taken at 800-443-ERIC or 703-440-1400.) When ordering, please specify the document (ED) number. Documents are available as noted in microfiche (MF) and paper copy (PC). If you have the price code ready when you call EDRS, an exact price can be quoted. The last page of the latest issue of *Resources in Education* also has the current cost, listed by code.

Adelman, Clifford. 1990. *A College Course Map.* Washington, D.C.: U.S. Department of Education, Office of Educational Research and Improvement. ED 326 153. 260 pp. MF–01; PC–11.

Afonso, Janet. 1990. "The International Dimension in American Higher Education." Doctoral dissertation, University of Arizona.

Altbach, Philip. 1991. "Patterns in Higher Education Development: Toward the Year 2000." *Review of Higher Education* 14(3): 293-316.

American Council on Education. 1984. *Guidelines for College and University Linkages Abroad.* Washington, D.C.: Author. ED 250 997. 24 pp. MF–01; PC–01.

———. November 1990. "Building East-West Partnerships: Helsinki Meeting Fosters Multi-Lateral Ties." *Higher Education and National Affairs.* Special report. Washington, D.C.

Anderson, Charles J. 1988. *International Studies for Undergraduates, 1987: Operations and Opinions.* Higher Education Report No. 76. Washington D.C.: American Council on Education.

Anderson, Lee. 1991. "A Rationale for Global Education." In *Global Education.* Kenneth Tye, ed. Arlington, Va.: Association for Supervision and Curriculum Development.

Arum, Stephen. 1987. *International Education: What Is It? A Taxonomy of International Education of U.S. Universities.* New York: Council on International Educational Exchange. Occasional Paper No. 23. ED 305 835. 28 pp. MF–01; PC–02.

Ashby, Eric. 1966. *Universities: British, Indian, African.* Cambridge, Mass.: Harvard University Press.

Astin, Alexander, et al. 1983. *The American Freshman: National Norms for Fall 1983.* Los Angeles: Higher Education Research Institute, University of California. ED 239 542. 220 pp. MF–01; PC–09.

———. 1986. *The American Freshman: National Norms for Fall*

1986. Los Angeles: Higher Education Research Institute, University of California. ED 278 296. 267 pp. MF–01; PC not available EDRS.

———. 1987. *The American Freshman: National Norms for Fall 1987.* Los Angeles: Higher Education Research Institute, University of California. ED 290 371. MF–01; PC not available EDRS.

Bachner, David, and Ulrich Zeutschel. 1990. *Students of Four Decades: Influences of an International Educational Exchange Experience on the Lives of German and U.S. High School Students.* Washington, D.C.: Youth For Understanding.

Backman, Earl L., ed. 1984. *Approaches to International Education.* New York: American Council on Education/Macmillan.

Barber, Elinor G., Philip G. Altbach, and Robert G. Meyers. 1984. *Bridges to Knowledge.* Chicago: The University of Chicago Press.

Bates, A.W. 1987. "The Organization and Management of a European Satellite System." ED 291 375. 18 pp. MF–01; PC–01.

Black, Robert, and George W. Bonham. 1981. "The Council on Learning Project on Education: Education and the World View." *Annals of the American Academy of Political Science* 449: 102-13.

Bozeman, Adda B. 1960. *Politics and Culture in International History.* Princeton, N.J.: Princeton University Press.

Brickman, William W. 1965. "Historical Development of Governmental Interest in International Higher Education." In *Governmental Policy in International Education.* S. Fraser, ed. New York: John Wiley.

Brown, Peggy Ann, ed. 1984. "Internationalizing the Curriculum." Washington, D.C.: Association of American Colleges. ED 242 239. 19 pp. MF–01; PC not available EDRS.

Brownlie, Ian. 1971. *Basic Documents on Human Rights.* Oxford: Clarendon.

Burn, Barbara. 1991. *Integrating Study Abroad into the Undergraduate Liberal Arts Curriculum: Eight Institutional Case Studies.* New York: Greenwood Press.

———, L. Cerych, and A. Smith, eds. 1990. Study Abroad Programmes. *Higher Education Policy Series* 11, vol. 1. London: Jessica Kingsley.

———, and Ralph Smuckler. 1990. *A National Mandate for Education Abroad: Getting on With the Task.* Washington, D.C.: National Association of Student Affairs.

Butts, R. Freeman. 1968. "America's Role in International Education: A Perspective on Thirty Years." In *The United States and International Education.* Harold G. Shane, ed. Chicago: National Society for the Study of Education. 68th yearbook, part 1: 3-45.

———, and L.C. Cremin. 1953. *A History of Education in American Culture.* New York: Holt, Rinehart, and Winston.

Carlson, Jerry S., Barbara Burn, John Useem, and David Yachimowicz. 1990. *Study Abroad: The Experience of American Undergraduates.* New York: Greenwood Press.

Cerych, Ladislav. 1991. "Higher Education and Europe After 1992."

European Education 23(2): 77-95.

Chambers, Gail S., and William K. Cummings. 1990. *Profiting from Education: Japan-United States International Education Ventures in the 1980s.* New York: Institute of International Education. Report No. 20. ED 320 488. 180 pp. MF–01; PC–08.

Chandler, Alice. 1989. *Obligation or Opportunity: Foreign Student Policy in Six Major Receiving Countries.* New York: Institute of International Education. Report No. 18. ED 312 981. 144 pp. MF–01; PC–06.

Chronicle of Higher Education. December 4, 1991: A55. Washington, D.C.

Clark, Burton. 1983. *The Higher Education System: Academic Organization in Cross-National Perspective.* Berkeley: UC Press.

Council on International Educational Exchange. 1992. *Black Students and Overseas Programs: Broadening the Base of Participation.* New York.

Cogan, John, Judith Torney-Purta, and Douglas Anderson. 1988. "Knowledge and Attitudes Toward Global Issues: Students in Japan and the United States." *Comparative Education Review* 32(3): 282-97.

Cole, Donna J., and Theresa McCormick. 1987. "Infusions of International Perspectives into Undergraduate Teacher Education Programs." ED 289 855. 21 pp. MF–01; PC–01.

Cole, Michael. 1990. "The World Beyond Our Borders: What Might Our Students Need to Know?" In *Group Portrait. Internationalizing the Disciplines.* Sven Groennings and David S. Wiley, eds. New York: The American Forum.

Coombs, Philip H. 1985. *The World Crisis in Education: The View From the Eighties.* New York: Oxford University Press. Council on International and Public Affairs. 1990. *International Studies Funding and Resources Book: The Education Interface Guide to Sources of Support for International Education.* 5th ed. New York: Apex Press.

Council on Learning. 1981. "1981 Questionnaire Worksheet for Program Planning and Evaluation in Foreign Language and International Studies." New Rochelle, N.Y.: *Change* Magazine Press.

Council on Postsecondary Accreditation. 1987. "Final Report of the Ad Hoc Committee on the Accreditation of Foreign Institutions and Programs." Washington, D.C.

Crawford-Lange, Linda, and Dale Lange. 1984. "Doing the Unthinkable in the Second-Language Classroom: A Process for the Integration of Language and Culture." In *Teaching for Proficiency, The Organizing Principle.* Theodore V. Higgs, ed. Lincolnwood, Ill.: National textbook.

Cressey, William W. 1991. "Georgetown University: The Articulation of Study-Abroad Programs and the Home Campus Curriculum." In *Integrating Study Abroad into the Undergraduate Liberal Arts*

Curriculum. Barbara Burn, ed. New York: Greenwood Press.

d'Almeida, Irene Assiba. 1982. "The Meaning and Status of International Studies in West African Schools." *Theory into Practice* 21(3): 193-99.

Dawson, Ian. 1989. "The Schools History Project—A Study in Curriculum Development. *The History Teacher* 22(3): 221-38.

Delaney, Jean. 1991. "The University of Colorado at Boulder: The International Affairs Major." In *Integrating Study Abroad into the Undergraduate Liberal Arts Curriculum.* Barbara Burn, ed. New York: Greenwood Press.

Demuth, Katherine A., and N.B. Smith. 1987. "The Foreign Language Requirement: An Alternative Program." *Foreign Language Annals* 20(1): 67-77.

Dinniman, Andrew, and Holzner Burkart, eds. 1988. *Education for International Competence in Pennsylvania.* Pennsylvania Dept. of Education and the University Center for International Studies, University of Pittsburgh.

Draper, Jamie B. 1989. *The States of the States: State Initiatives in Foreign Languages and International Studies, 1979-1989.* Washington, D.C.: Joint National Committee for Languages.

Ebuchi, Kazuhiro. 1989. "Foreign Students and Internationalization of the University: A View from Japanese Perspective." In *Research Institute for Higher Education* (eds.), *Foreign Students and Internationalization of Higher Education.* Hiroshima: Hiroshima University.

———. 1991. "The Effects of Governmental Policies on Foreign Students in Japan: A Brief Statement of General Policy Trends." *Higher Education* 21: 407-22.

Edmondson, Locksley. 1984. "Black American Educational Interests in the Era of Globalism." *Journal of Negro Education* 53(3): 243-56.

Education and World Affairs. 1965. *The University Looks Abroad: Approaches to World Affairs at Six American Universities.* New York: Walker.

Encyclopedia of Educational Research. 1982. Harry Mitzel, John Best, and William Rabinowitz, eds. From *International Education* 2: 945-58.

Encyclopedia of Higher Education. 1991. Burton R. Clark and Guy Neave, eds. Vols. 1-4. New York: Pergamon Press.

Engerman, David, and Parker Marden. 1992. *In the International Interest: Contributions and Needs of America's Liberal Arts Colleges.* Beloit, Wis.: Beloit College.

Enklaar, Hans. 1985. "International Education: The Dutch System." *Western European Education* 17(1): 46-62.

Eurich, Nell P. 1981. *Systems of Higher Education in Twelve Countries: A Comparative View.* New York: Praeger.

European Center for Higher Education. 1987. *Bibliography of Avail-*

*able Literature Relating to the Recognition of Studies, Diplomas,
and Degrees and to International Mobility in Higher Education.*
Bucharest, UNESCO: European Center for Higher Education. ED
292 428. 122 pp. MF–01; PC–05.

Flint, William. 1989. *Modern Technology in Foreign Language Education: Applications and Projects.* Lincolnwood, Ill.: National
Textbook.

Ford Foundation. 1976. *International Studies in Six European Countries: United Kingdom, France, Federal Republic of Germany,
Sweden, The Netherlands, Italy.* New York.

Fox, Elizabeth. 1985. "International Schools and the International
Baccalaureate." *Harvard Educational Review* 55(1): 53-68.

Frankel, Charles. 1965. *The Neglected Aspect of Foreign Affairs: American Educational and Cultural Policy Abroad.* Washington, D.C.:
The Brookings Institute.

Freed, Barbara. 1989. "Perspectives on the Future of Proficiency-
Based Teaching and Testing." *ADFL Bulletin* 20(2): 52-57.

Freeman, Jennifer. 1987. "The International Baccalaureate." *College
Board Review* 143: 4-6.

Garg, Ramesh C. 1987. "How to Internationalize the Finance Curriculum." In *Languages and Communications for World Business
and the Professions Conference Proceedings.* ED 293 310. 23 pp.
MF–01; PC–01.

Goodman, Neal R., J. Michael Armer, and Susan Carlson, eds. 1991.
Internationalizing the Sociology Curriculum: Syllabi and Resources.
2d ed. Washington, D.C.: American Sociological Association.

Goodrich, L.M., E. Hambro, and A.P. Simons. 1969. *Charter of the
United Nations.* 3rd ed. New York: Columbia University Press.

Goodwin, C.D., and Michael Nacht. 1983. *Absence of Decision: For-
eign Students in American Colleges and Universities.* New York:
Institute of International Education. ED 234 492. 58 pp. MF–01;
PC–03.

———. 1988. *Abroad and Beyond: Patterns in American Overseas
Education.* New York: Cambridge University Press.

———. 1991. *Missing the Boat: The Failure to Internalize American
Higher Education.* New York: Cambridge University Press.

Greene, William. 1985. "The International/Intercultural General Education Requirement." *Community and Junior College Journal*
55(4): 18-23.

Groennings, Sven, and David S. Wiley, eds. 1990. *Group Portrait:
Internationalizing the Disciplines.* New York: The American Forum.

Gueulette, David G. 1987. "Internationalizing Teacher Education:
The Northern Illinois University Plan." Netherlands: Paper presented at the World Assembly of the International Council on Education for Teaching. ED 248 862. 15 pp. MF–01; PC–01.

Gutek, Gerald L. 1985. *Internationalizing the Social Foundations
of Education.* Chicago: Loyola University of Chicago. ED 265 103.

20 pp. MF–01; PC–01.

Haggenbloom, Steven. 1989. "Teaching About Human Rights." In Thomas and Klare (eds.), *Peace and World Order Studies*. Boulder, Colo.: Westview Press.

Hammond, Grant T. 1989. "The State of Undergraduate Education in International Relations." *Political Science Teacher* 2(1): 1-4.

Harari, Maurice. 1983. *Internationalizing the Curriculum and the Campus: Guidelines for the AASCU Institutions*. Washington, D.C.: American Association of State Colleges and Universities. ED 212 244. 65 pp. MF–01. PC not available EDRS.

Harf, James, and Chadwick Alger. 1985. "Global Education: Why? For Whom? About What?" Columbus: The Mershon Center, The Ohio State University. ED 265 107. 30 pp. MF–01; PC–02.

Hayden, Rose. 1980. "U.S. Government Exchanges: The Quest for Coordination." *The Annals of the American Academy of Political and Social Science* 449: 114-28.

———. 1982. International Studies Goals. In *International Role of the Universities of the Eighties*. Michigan State University.

Healy, Lynn M. (N.D.) *Introducing International Development Content in the Social Work Curriculum*. Silver Spring, Md.: National Association of Social Workers.

Henderson, Ingeborg. 1983. "The Undergraduate Internship in the Foreign Language Curriculum." *Foreign Language Annals* 16(2): 99-102.

Henson, James, Jan Noel, Thomas Gillard-Byers, and Marcus Ingle. 1990. "Internationalizing U.S. Universities-Preliminary Summary of a National Study." In *Internationalizing U.S. Universities Conference Proceedings*. June 5-7, 1990. Spokane: International Program Development Office, Washington State University.

"History of Education." 1985. *Encyclopedia Brittanica* 18: 11-100. Chicago.

Hook, Glen. 1989. "Internationalization of Contemporary Japan." *The Japan Foundation Newsletter* 17(1): 13-16.

Hoopes, David S., ed. 1984. *Global Guide to International Education*. New York: Facts on File.

IAU Bulletin. April, June, August 1990. Paris: International Universities Bulletin.

International Encyclopedia of Comparative Higher Education. 1991. New York: Garland Publishing.

International Encyclopedia of Education. 1985. T. Husen and T.N. Postlethwaite, eds. Vol. 4. New York: Pergamon Press.

Jackson, Sir Gordon. 1984. "Report of the Committee to Review the Australian Overseas Aid Program." Canberra: Australian Government.

Janes, Jackson, and Helene Scher. 1987. *Mixed Messages: A Report on the Study of Contemporary Germany in the United States*. Washington, D.C.: German Marshall Fund for the United States.

Japan Foundation. 1989. *Japanese Studies in the United States.* Vols.
1-2. Ann Arbor, Mich.: Association for Asian Studies.

Jenkins, Hugh M., and Associates. 1983. *Educating Students From
Other Nations.* San Francisco: Jossey-Bass.

Jurasek, Richard. 1988. "Integrating Foreign Languages into the College Curriculum." *Modern Language Journal* 72: 52-58.

————. 1991. "Earlham College: Connecting Off-Campus and On-
Campus Learning." In *Integrating Study Abroad into the Under-
graduate Liberal Arts Curriculum.* Barbara Burn, ed. New York:
Greenwood Press.

Kandel, Isaac L. 1944. *Intellectual Cooperation: National and International.* New York: Teachers College Bureau of Publication.

Keohane, Robert O. 1990. "Teaching How to ask Questions About
International Relations." In *Group Portrait: Internationalizing
the Disciplines.* Sven Groennings and David Wiley, eds. New York:
The American Forum.

Kitamura, Kazuyuki. May 1983. "The Internalization of Higher Education in Japan." *The Japan Foundation Newsletter* 1-9.

Klinger, M. Robert. 1965. "The Development of the National Asso-
ciation for Foreign Student Affairs From Idea to Institution." In
Governmental Policy and Education. Stewart Fraser, ed. New York:
John Wiley.

Klitgaard, Robert. 1981. "Why International Studies." *Change* Jan/
Feb: 28-34.

Kobayashi, Tetsuya. 1979. "The Internationalization of Japanese
Higher Education." In *Changes in the Japanese University: A Com-
parative Perspective.* William Cummings, Ikuo Amano, and
Kazayuki Kitamura, eds. New York: Praeger.

Kyllonen, Timo. 1984. "Internationalism and Finnish Higher Education." *Higher Education in Europe* 9(2): 50-56.

Lafayette, Robert C. 1985. "Education Theory and Methods: Inter-
national Teacher Education." Paper commissioned by the American
Association of Colleges for Teacher Education for the International
Teacher Education Project. ED 265 104. 22 pp. MF–01; PC–01.

Lambert, Richard D. 1980. "International Studies: An Overview and
Agenda." *The Annals of the American Academy of Political and
Social Science* 449: 151-64.

————. 1986. *Points of Leverage: An Agenda for a National Foundation for International Studies.* New York: Social Science
Research Council.

————. 1989. *International Studies and the Undergraduate.*
Washington D.C.: American Council on Education.

Lamy, Stephen L. 1987. *The Definition of a Discipline: The Objects
and Methods of Analysis in Global Education.* New York: Global
Perspectives in Education Occasional Paper.

Laribee, Stephen F. 1988. "International Accounting and the Accounting Educator." In *Proceedings of the Seventh Annual Eastern Mich-*

igan University Conference on Languages for Business and the Professions. ED 304 897. 18 pp. MF–01; PC–01.

Laroche, Jacque. 1985. "Undergraduate Internship in Conversation." *Foreign Language Annals* 18(3): 209-12.

Laves, Walter H., and C.A. Thomson. 1957. *UNESCO.* Bloomington: Indiana University Press.

Leaver, Betty Lou, and S.B. Stryker. 1989. "Content-Based Instruction for Foreign Language Classrooms." *Foreign Language Annals* 22(3): 269-75.

Leestma, Robert. 1969. "OE's Institute of International Studies." *American Education*: 5-8.

———. 1981. "Comparative and International Education in the U.S. Office of Education: A Bibliography of Studies and Publications, 1968-1980." *Comparative Education Review*: 272-88.

Leinwald, Gerald. 1983. *Without A Nickel: The Challenge of Internationalizing the Curriculum and the Campus.* Washington, D.C.: American Association of State Colleges and Universities.

Lewis, Samuel. 1989. "The United States Institute for Peace: A New Federal Role in Peace Education and Research. *COPRED Peace Chronicle* 14(1): 5.

Liaison Group for International Educational Exchange. 1989. *Exchange 2000: International Leadership for the Next Century.* Washington, D.C.

Lopez, George. 1989. "Conceptual Models for Peace Studies Programs." In Thomas and Klare, *Peace and World Order Studies.* Boulder, Colo.: Westview Press.

———. 1989. "Trends in College Curricula and Programs." *Annals of the American Academy of Political and Social Science* 504: 9-13.

Lulat, Y. G-M. 1987. Comparative International Education Bibliography. *Comparative Education Review* 31(3): 442-58.

Lulat, Y. G-M., and P. Altbach. 1985. "International Students in Comparative Perspective." In John Smart (ed.), *Higher Education: Handbook of Theory and Research.* New York: Agathon Press.

Luttikholt, Harry. 1987. "EEC Sources of Support for Higher Education and Research in 1988." *CRE--Information* 80: 83-103.

McCarthy, Joann. 1986. "Internationalizing the Curriculum." Washington, D.C.: American Association of State Colleges and Universities. ED 306 854. 48 pp. MF–01; PC–02.

McCaughey, Robert. 1984. *International Studies and Academic Enterprise.* New York: Columbia University Press.

McLean, John J. 1990. "Consortial Approaches to Education." In Richard Greenfield (ed.), *Developing International Education Programs.* New Directions for Community Colleges No. 70, 18(2): 47-56. San Francisco: Jossey-Bass.

Marshall, Terry L. 1987. "The Multi-Language Seminar: An Approach to Offering More of the 'Less Commonly Taught' Languages." *For-*

eign Language Annals 20(2): 155-63.

Mashiko, Ellen. 1989. *Japan.* World Education Series. Washington, D.C.: American Association of Collegiate Registrars and Admission Officers.

Mayhew, Paula. 1990. "Overview of International Educational Initiatives in the Middle States Region." Philadelphia, Pa.: Middle States Commission on Higher Education.

Merryfield, Merry. 1991. "Preparing American Secondary Social Studies Teachers to Teach with a Global Perspective: A Status Report." *Journal of Teacher Education* 42(1): 11-20.

Moeller, Paulette. 1989. "The Making of a Foreign Language Teacher—Regina Style." *Foreign Language Annals* 22(2): 135-44.

Morgenthau, Hans. 1967. *Politics Among Nations.* 4th ed. New York: Knopf.

Nagai, Michio. 1980. "Higher Education in an Age of Internationalization." In Hiroshima University Research Institute for Higher Education, *Higher Education in the 1980s: Challenges and Responses.*

National Endowment for the Humanities. 1988, 1989. *Foreign Language Programs Funded in Higher Education.* Washington, D.C.: National Endowment for the Humanities.

National Endowment for the Humanities. 1991. *National Tests: What Other Countries Expect Their Students to Know.* Washington, D.C.

National Governors Association. 1989. *America In Transition, The International Frontier: Report of the Task Force on International Education.* Washington, D.C.: National Governors Association. ED 316 447. 89 pp. MF–01. PC not available EDRS.

Natoli, Salvatore J., and Andrew R. Bond, eds. 1985. "Geography in Internationalizing the Undergraduate Curriculum." Washington D.C.: American Association of Geographers.

Neave, Guy. 1989. "On Articulating Secondary School, Higher Education and 1992." *European Journal of Education* 24(4): 351-63.

Newell, Barbara. 1987. "Education with a World Perspective: A Necessity for America's Political and Economic Defense." *Annals of the American Academy of Political and Social Sciences* 491: 134ff.

Ochoa, Ann. 1986. "Reforming Preservice Education: An International Dimension." Indiana: Social Studies Development Center. ED 298 130. 35 pp. MF–01; PC–02.

Opper, S., U. Teichler, and J. Carlson. 1990. "The Impact of Study-Abroad Programmes on Students and Graduates." Higher Education Policy Series 11, vol. 2. London: Jessica Kingsley.

Palmer, Norman. 1980. "The Study of International Relations in the United States: Perspective of Half a Century." *International Studies Quarterly* 24(3): 343-64.

Pankenier, David. December 5, 1990. "Foreign Language Requirements at the College Level Do Not Work." *Chronicle of Higher*

Education 37(14): B1-B53.

Pelton, Joseph N. 1987. "A New Era Begins: Satellite Communications and Development." Arlie, Va.: Paper presented at the Telecommunications Research Policy Conference. ED 289 457. 19 pp. MF–01; PC–01.

Peterson, A.D.C. 1972. *The International Baccalaureate*. London: George Harrap.

Pickert, Sarah, and Barbara Turlington. 1992. *Internationalizing the Undergraduate Curriculum: A Handbook for Campus Leaders*. Washington, D.C.: American Council on Education.

Pike, L.W., T.S. Barrows, M.H. Mahoney, and A. Jugeblut. 1979. *Other Nations, Other People: A Survey of Student Interests, Knowledge, Attitudes, and Perceptions*. Washington D.C.: U.S. Government Printing Office. ED 189 190. 177 pp. MF–01; PC–08.

President's Commission on Foreign Language and International Studies. 1979. *Strength Through Wisdom: A Critique of U.S. Capability*. Washington D.C.: U.S. Government Printing Office. ED 176 599. 161 pp. MF–01; PC–07.

Ramaglia, Judith. 1988. "Internationalizing the Introductory Accounting Course: A Case History of the Nitty Gritty." In *Proceedings of the Seventh Annual Eastern Michigan University Conference on Languages for Business and the Professions*. ED 304 896. 30 pp. MF–01; PC–02.

Reilly, Kevin. 1985. *World History: Selected Reading Lists and Course Outlines From American Colleges and Universities*. New York: M. Wiener.

Rothney, John. August 1987. "Developing the Twentieth Century World History Course: A Case Study at Ohio State." *History Teacher* 20(4): 465-85.

Sakamoto, Clyde, and Mary F. Field, eds. 1987. *The Next Challenge: Balancing International Competition and Cooperation*. Washington, D.C.: American Association of Community and Junior Colleges. ED 280 058. 104 pp. MF–01; PC– 05.

Scanlon, David. 1960. *International Education: A Documentary Listing*. New York: Teachers College Press.

Southern Governors Association. 1986. *Findings of the Southern Governors Association Advisory Council*. Gerald Baliles, Governor of Virginia, Chairman.

Spaulding, Seth, and Michael Flack. 1976. *The World's Students in the U.S.: A Review and Evaluation of Research on Foreign Students*. New York: Praeger.

Stein, Todd J. 1990. "Foreign Educational Programs in Britain: Legal Issues Associated with Establishment and Taxation of Programs Abroad." *Journal of College and University Law* 16(3): 521-45.

Thomas, Daniel, and Michael Klare. 1989. *Peace and World Order Studies*. Boulder, Colo.: Westview Press.

Thomas, R. Murray, ed. 1990. *International Comparative Education*.

New York: Pergamon Press.

Tiryakian, Edward A. 1990. "Sociology's Great Leap Forward: The Challenge of Internationalization." In Sven Groennings and David Wiley, eds., *Group Portrait: Internationalizing the Disciplines*. New York: The American Forum.

Tonkin, Humphrey, and Jane Edwards. 1981. *The World in the Curriculum: Curricular Strategies for the 21st Century*. New York: *Change* Magazine Press.

Torney-Purta, Judith. 1977. "International Knowledge and Awareness of Adolescents in Nine Countries." *International Journal of Political Education* 1: 3-19.

———. 1989. "Measuring the Effectiveness of World Studies Courses." In *Approaches to World Studies: A Handbook for Curriculum Planning*. Robert Woyach and Richard Remy, eds. Boston: Allyn and Bacon.

———. 1990. "Annotated Bibliography of Materials to Add an International Dimension to Undergraduate Courses in Developmental and Social Psychology. In *Group Portrait: Internationalizing the Disciplines*. Sven Groennings and David Wiley, eds. New York: The American Forum.

———. October 1990. "International Comparative Research in Education: Its Role in Educational Improvement in the U.S." *Educational Researcher*. 32-35.

Tucker, Jan. 1991. "Global Education Partnerships Between Schools and Universities." In *Global Education*. 1991 Yearbook of the Association for Supervision and Curriculum Development. Kenneth A. Tye, ed. Arlington, Va.: 109-24.

U.S. Department of Education. Fund for the Improvement of Postsecondary Education (FIPSE). 1986; 1987; 1988; 1989; 1990. *Comprehensive Program Project Descriptions*. Washington, D.C.

U.S. Department of Education. 1984. *Japanese Education Today*. Washington, D.C.

U.S. Department of Education. Title VI Higher Education Act. 1986; 1987; 1988. Undergraduate International Students and Foreign Language Program. *Project Abstracts*. Washington, D.C.: U.S. Department of Education.

———. Part B of the Higher Education Act. 1987-88; 1988-89; 1989-90. *Business and International Education Program Project Abstracts*. Washington, D.C.: U.S. Department of Education.

Van Dijk, Hans. 1985. "The Study Assessment Division of the Netherlands Universities Foundation for International Cooperation." *Higher Education in Europe* 10(2): 118-21.

Van Els, T.J.M. 1988. "Towards a Foreign Language Teaching Policy for the European Community: A Dutch Perspective." *Language, Culture, and Curriculum* 1(1): 53-65.

Veysey, L.R. 1973. *The Emergence of the American University*. Chicago: University of Chicago Press.

Vocke, David. 1988. "What is Global Education?" *The Social Studies*. January/February 1988: 18-20.

Walberg, Herbert. 1990. "OECD Indicators of Educational Productivity." *Educational Researcher* June/July 1990: 30-33.

Wallerstein, Immanuel. 1990. Sociology for Undergraduates: Social Systems as World Systems. In *Group Portrait: Internationalizing the Disciplines*. Sven Groennings and David Wiley, eds. New York: The American Forum.

West, Bradley B. 1985. "The State of the Profession: International Field/Student Teaching Experiences in Undergraduate Teacher Preparation." Michigan State University, College of Education. ED 265 113. 31 pp. MF–01; PC–02.

Wien, Barbara. 1981. *Peace and World Order Studies: A Curriculum Guide* 1(2). New York: World Policy Institute.

Wilkenfeld, Jonathan. 1983. "Computer Assisted International Studies." *Teaching Political Science* 10(4): 171-76.

Will, W. Marvin. 1980. "American Politics in Comparative Perspective: Thoughts on Teaching the Course to International Students." *Teaching Political Science* 7(4): 473-80.

Yearbook of International Organizations: 1989-1990. Union of International Associations, ed. Vol. 1, 26th ed. New York: K.G. Saur.

Zikopoulos, M., ed. 1988. *Open Doors 1987-1988: Report on International Exchange*. New York: Institute of International Education. ED 303 117. 189 pp. MF–01; PC–08.

———. 1989. *Open Doors 1988-1989: Report on International Exchange*. New York: Institute of International Education. ED 316 162. 217 pp. MF–01. PC not available EDRS.

———. 1991. *Open Doors 1990-1991: Report on International Exchange*. New York: Institute of International Education. ED 340 324. 194 pp. MF–01; PC–08.

Zimmern, Alfred. 1939. *The League of Nations and the Rule of Law 1937-1935*. New York: Russell & Russell.

INDEX

A

Agency for International Development, 5
        Center for University Cooperation in Development, 6
Alexander the Great, 1
American Academy of Political and Social Science, 21
American Association of State Colleges and Universities, 49
American Council on Education, 48, 57
        survey, 53
American Field Service, 33
American Sociological Association, 18
Asoka the Great, 1
Associated Colleges of the Midwest, 51
Associated Colleges of the Twin Cities, 51
Association of International Education Administrators, 47

B

Bologna, University of, founding, 2
Boston University
        language training, 14
British Education Reform Act, 56
Brown University
        foreign languages, 16

C

California State University, 22
California, University of, San Diego, 31
Canada
        international education, 8
Carnegie, Andrew, 3
Carter, Jimmy, 6
Center for International Business Education
        funding, 6
Chronicle of Higher Education, 11
Clemson University
        language training, 14
Cold War, 4
Colorado School of Mines, 23
Colorado, University of, 34
Commission on Foreign Language and International Studies, 6
Commission on Postsecondary Accreditation, 55
Convention on the Recognition of Studies, Degrees, and Diplomas
        UNESCO, 43
Council on International Educational Exchange, 30
Council on Learning, 25, 52
Cross culture
        students, 33
Crosscultural communication, 63

Curriculum
>foreign students, 25
>international focus, 17
>reform, 11, 62, 66

D

Debriefing programs
>students abroad, 63
Dickinson College, 36
Dominican Association for Self-Study and Accreditation, 56

E

Earlham College, 36
>foreign study, 15, 16, 34
Education majors
>international studies, 23
Education, Department of, 5, 54
Educational mobility, 67
>American strengths, 44
>American weaknesses, 44
>research, 44
Educational Testing Service, 25
ERIC Clearinghouse on Higher Education, 57
Ethnic studies, 21
European Center for Higher Education, 65
European colleges and universities
>cooperative arrangements, 57
European Community Action Scheme for the Mobility of University Students (ERASMUS), 41
European Community Course Credit Transfer System (ECTS), 41
Exchange programs
>international, 1

F

Florida International University, 23
Ford Foundation, 5, 20
Foreign language departments
>foreign cultures, 18
Foreign language requirements
>public schools, 13
Foreign language study
>colleges and universities, 12
Foreign Service Institute, 13
Foreign student admissions
>policies, 45
Foreign students, 29, 37
>Australia, 40
>Canada, 40

K
Kalamazoo College, 35, 36
Kellogg, W.W., 3

L
Lafayette College, 23
Language instruction
        European Community, 43
        satellite broadcasting, 19
Language mentors, 37
League of Nations, 2
        Committee on Intellectual Cooperation, 3
Lehigh University
        language training, 14
Lewis and Clark College
        overseas study, 15

M
Marshall Plan, 4
Maryland, University of, 24
        foreign languages, 19
Michigan, University of
        School of Business Administration, 22
Middle States Commission on Higher Education, 56
Minnesota, University of
        Russian studies, 51
Montpellier, University of
        founding, 2
Multinational exchanges, 46

N
National Council on Foreign Language and International
    Studies, 17
National Defense Education Act, 5
National Endowment for the Humanities, 5, 12, 14, 27
National Governors Association, 7
National Security Education Act, 6, 66
National Student Association for Foreign Student Affairs, 3
Netherlands Universities Foundation for International
    Cooperation, 8
New York, State University of, 20
North Carolina, University of, 16
Northern Illinois University, 23

O
Ohio State University, 15
Oregon State University
        international studies, 16

Trans-Regional Academic Mobility and Credential Evaluation
(TRACE), 41
Treaties of Westphalia, 2

U

U.S. programs abroad
accreditation, 55
UNESCO, 3, 4, 57, 58, 65
journal, 11
United States Institute of Peace, 21

V

Virginia Tidewater Consortium for Higher Education, 51
Virginia, University of
founding, 2

W

Wageningen Agricultural University, 8
Washington, University of, 4
William and Mary, College of
founding, 2

Y

Yale University, 2
Youth for Understanding, 33

ASHE-ERIC HIGHER EDUCATION REPORTS

Since 1983, the Association for the Study of Higher Education (ASHE) and the Educational Resources Information Center (ERIC) Clearinghouse on Higher Education, a sponsored project of the School of Education and Human Development at The George Washington University, have cosponsored the *ASHE-ERIC Higher Education Report* series. The 1992 series is the twenty-first overall and the fourth to be published by the School of Education and Human Development at the George Washington University.

Each monograph is the definitive analysis of a tough higher education problem, based on thorough research of pertinent literature and institutional experiences. Topics are identified by a national survey. Noted practitioners and scholars are then commissioned to write the reports, with experts providing critical reviews of each manuscript before publication.

Eight monographs (10 before 1985) in the ASHE-ERIC Higher Education Report series are published each year and are available on individual and subscription bases. Subscription to eight issues is $90.00 annually; $70 to members of AAHE, AIR, or AERA; and $60 to ASHE members. All foreign subscribers must include an additional $10 per series year for postage.

To order single copies of existing reports, use the order form on the last page of this book. Regular prices, and special rates available to members of AAHE, AIR, AERA and ASHE, are as follows:

Series	Regular	Members
1990 to 92	$17.00	$12.75
1988 and 89	15.00	11.25
1985 to 87	10.00	7.50
1983 and 84	7.50	6.00
before 1983	6.50	5.00

Price includes book rate postage within the U.S. For foreign orders, please add $1.00 per book. Fast United Parcel Service available within the contiguous U.S. at $2.50 for each order under $50.00, and calculated at 5% of invoice total for orders $50.00 or above.

All orders under $45.00 must be prepaid. Make check payable to ASHE-ERIC. For Visa or MasterCard, include card number, expiration date and signature. A bulk discount of 10% is available on orders of 10 or more books, and 40% on orders of 25 or more books (not applicable on subscriptions).

Address order to
ASHE-ERIC Higher Education Reports
The George Washington University
1 Dupont Circle, Suite 630
Washington, DC 20036
Or phone (202) 296-2597
Write or call for a complete catalog.

1992 ASHE-ERIC Higher Education Reports

1. The Leadership Compass: Values and Ethics in Higher Education
   by John R. Wilcox and Susan L. Ebbs

1991 ASHE-ERIC Higher Education Reports

1. Active Learning: Creating Excitement in the Classroom
   Charles C. Bonwell and James A. Eison

2. Realizing Gender Equality in Higher Education: The Need to Integrate Work/Family Issues
   Nancy Hensel

3. Academic Advising for Student Success: A System of Shared Responsibility
   by Susan H. Frost

4. Cooperative Learning: Increasing College Faculty Instructional Productivity
   by David W. Johnson, Roger T. Johnson, and Karl A. Smith

5. High School–College Partnerships: Conceptual Models, Programs, and Issues
   by Arthur Richard Greenberg

6. Meeting the Mandate: Renewing the College and Departmental Curriculum
   by William Toombs and William Tierney

7. Faculty Collaboration: Enhancing the Quality of Scholarship and Teaching
   by Ann E. Austin and Roger G. Baldwin

8. Strategies and Consequences: Managing the Costs in Higher Education
   by John S. Waggaman

1990 ASHE-ERIC Higher Education Reports

1. The Campus Green: Fund Raising in Higher Education
   Barbara E. Brittingham and Thomas R. Pezzullo

2. The Emeritus Professor: Old Rank - New Meaning
   James E. Mauch, Jack W. Birch, and Jack Matthews

3. "High Risk" Students in Higher Education: Future Trends
   Dionne J. Jones and Betty Collier Watson

4. Budgeting for Higher Education at the State Level: Enigma, Paradox, and Ritual
   Daniel T. Layzell and Jan W. Lyddon

5. Proprietary Schools: Programs, Policies, and Prospects
   John B. Lee and Jamie P. Merisotis

6. College Choice: Understanding Student Enrollment Behavior
   Michael B. Paulsen

7. Pursuing Diversity: Recruiting College Minority Students
   Barbara Astone and Elsa Nuñez-Wormack

8. Social Consciousness and Career Awareness: Emerging Link
   in Higher Education
   John S. Swift, Jr.

1989 ASHE-ERIC Higher Education Reports

1. Making Sense of Administrative Leadership: The 'L' Word in
   Higher Education
   Estela M. Bensimon, Anna Neumann, and Robert Birnbaum

2. Affirmative Rhetoric, Negative Action: African-American and
   Hispanic Faculty at Predominantly White Universities
   Valora Washington and William Harvey

3. Postsecondary Developmental Programs: A Traditional Agenda
   with New Imperatives
   Louise M. Tomlinson

4. The Old College Try: Balancing Athletics and Academics in
   Higher Education
   John R. Thelin and Lawrence L. Wiseman

5. The Challenge of Diversity: Involvement or Alienation in the
   Academy?
   Daryl G. Smith

6. Student Goals for College and Courses: A Missing Link in Assessing and Improving Academic Achievement
   Joan S. Stark, Kathleen M. Shaw, and Malcolm A. Lowther

7. The Student as Commuter: Developing a Comprehensive Institutional Response
   Barbara Jacoby

8. Renewing Civic Capacity: Preparing College Students for Service
   and Citizenship
   Suzanne W. Morse

1988 ASHE-ERIC Higher Education Reports

1. The Invisible Tapestry: Culture in American Colleges and
   Universities
   George D. Kuh and Elizabeth J. Whitt

2. Critical Thinking: Theory, Research, Practice, and Possibilities
   Joanne Gainen Kurfiss

3. Developing Academic Programs: The Climate for Innovation
   Daniel T. Seymour

4. Peer Teaching: To Teach is To Learn Twice
   Neal A. Whitman

---

5. Higher Education and State Governments: Renewed Partnership, Cooperation, or Competition?
   Edward R. Hines

6. Entrepreneurship and Higher Education: Lessons for Colleges, Universities, and Industry
   James S. Fairweather

7. Planning for Microcomputers in Higher Education: Strategies for the Next Generation
   Reynolds Ferrante, John Hayman, Mary Susan Carlson, and Harry Phillips

8. The Challenge for Research in Higher Education: Harmonizing Excellence and Utility
   Alan W. Lindsay and Ruth T. Neumann

1987 ASHE-ERIC Higher Education Reports

1. Incentive Early Retirement Programs for Faculty: Innovative Responses to a Changing Environment
   Jay L. Chronister and Thomas R. Kepple, Jr.

2. Working Effectively with Trustees: Building Cooperative Campus Leadership
   Barbara E. Taylor

3. Formal Recognition of Employer-Sponsored Instruction: Conflict and Collegiality in Postsecondary Education
   Nancy S. Nash and Elizabeth M. Hawthorne

4. Learning Styles: Implications for Improving Educational Practices
   Charles S. Claxton and Patricia H. Murrell

5. Higher Education Leadership: Enhancing Skills through Professional Development Programs
   Sharon A. McDade

6. Higher Education and the Public Trust: Improving Stature in Colleges and Universities
   Richard L. Alfred and Julie Weissman

7. College Student Outcomes Assessment: A Talent Development Perspective
   Maryann Jacobi, Alexander Astin, and Frank Ayala, Jr.

8. Opportunity from Strength: Strategic Planning Clarified with Case Examples
   Robert G. Cope

1986 ASHE-ERIC Higher Education Reports

1. Post-tenure Faculty Evaluation: Threat or Opportunity?
   Christine M. Licata

2. Blue Ribbon Commissions and Higher Education: Changing Academe from the Outside
   Janet R. Johnson and Laurence R. Marcus

3. Responsive Professional Education: Balancing Outcomes and Opportunities
   Joan S. Stark, Malcolm A. Lowther, and Bonnie M.K. Hagerty

4. Increasing Students' Learning: A Faculty Guide to Reducing Stress among Students
   Neal A. Whitman, David C. Spendlove, and Claire H. Clark

5. Student Financial Aid and Women: Equity Dilemma?
   Mary Moran

6. The Master's Degree: Tradition, Diversity, Innovation
   Judith S. Glazer

7. The College, the Constitution, and the Consumer Student: Implications for Policy and Practice
   Robert M. Hendrickson and Annette Gibbs

8. Selecting College and University Personnel: The Quest and the Question
   Richard A. Kaplowitz

1985 ASHE-ERIC Higher Education Reports

1. Flexibility in Academic Staffing: Effective Policies and Practices
   Kenneth P. Mortimer, Marque Bagshaw, and Andrew T. Masland

2. Associations in Action: The Washington, D.C. Higher Education Community
   Harland G. Bloland

3. And on the Seventh Day: Faculty Consulting and Supplemental Income
   Carol M. Boyer and Darrell R. Lewis

4. Faculty Research Performance: Lessons from the Sciences and Social Sciences
   John W. Creswell

5. Academic Program Review: Institutional Approaches, Expectations, and Controversies
   Clifton F. Conrad and Richard F. Wilson

6. Students in Urban Settings: Achieving the Baccalaureate Degree
   Richard C. Richardson, Jr. and Louis W. Bender

7. Serving More Than Students: A Critical Need for College Student Personnel Services
   Peter H. Garland

8. Faculty Participation in Decision Making: Necessity or Luxury?
   Carol E. Floyd

1984 ASHE-ERIC Higher Education Reports

1. Adult Learning: State Policies and Institutional Practices
   K. Patricia Cross and Anne-Marie McCartan

2. Student Stress: Effects and Solutions
   Neal A. Whitman, David C. Spendlove, and Claire H. Clark

3. Part-time Faulty: Higher Education at a Crossroads
   Judith M. Gappa

4. Sex Discrimination Law in Higher Education: The Lessons of the Past Decade. ED 252 169.*
   J. Ralph Lindgren, Patti T. Ota, Perry A. Zirkel, and Nan Van Gieson

5. Faculty Freedoms and Institutional Accountability: Interactions and Conflicts
   Steven G. Olswang and Barbara A. Lee

6. The High Technology Connection: Academic/Industrial Cooperation for Economic Growth
   Lynn G. Johnson

7. Employee Educational Programs: Implications for Industry and Higher Education. ED 258 501.*
   Suzanne W. Morse

8. Academic Libraries: The Changing Knowledge Centers of Colleges and Universities
   Barbara B. Moran

9. Futures Research and the Strategic Planning Process: Implications for Higher Education
   James L. Morrison, William L. Renfro, and Wayne I. Boucher

10. Faculty Workload: Research, Theory, and Interpretation
    Harold E. Yuker

*Out-of-print. Available through EDRS. Call 1-800-443-ERIC.

Quantity Amount

———— Please begin my subscription to the 1992 *ASHE-ERIC Higher Education Reports* at $90.00, 33% off the cover price, starting with Report 1, 1992. ————

———— Please send a complete set of the 1991 *ASHE-ERIC Higher Education Reports* at $80.00, 41% off the cover price. ————

———— Outside the U.S., add $10.00 per series for postage. ————

Individual reports are avilable at the following prices:

1990 and 1991, $17.00	1983 and 1984, $7.50
1988 and 1989, $15.00	1982 and back, $6.50
1985 to 1987, $10.00	

Book rate postage within the U.S. is included. Outside U.S., please add $1.00 per book for postage. Fast U.P.S. shipping is available within the contiguous U.S. at $2.50 for each order under $50.00, and calculated at 5% of invoice total for orders $50.00 or above. All orders under $45.00 must be prepaid.

PLEASE SEND ME THE FOLLOWING REPORTS:

Quantity	Report No.	Year	Title	Amount

Subtotal:	
Foreign or UPS:	
Total Due:	

Please check one of the following:
☐ Check enclosed, payable to GWU-ERIC.
☐ Purchase order attached ($45.00 minimum).
☐ Charge my credit card indicated below:
  ☐ Visa   ☐ MasterCard

Expiration Date ——————

Name ——————————————————————————

Title ——————————————————————————

Institution ——————————————————————

Address ————————————————————————

City ———————————————— State ———— Zip ————

Phone ——————————————————————————

Signature ———————————————— Date ————

SEND ALL ORDERS TO:
ASHE-ERIC Higher Education Reports
The George Washington University
One Dupont Circle, Suite 630
Washington, DC 20036-1183
Phone: (202) 296-2597